Hard Press

THE CONQUEST OF THE OLD SOUTHWEST: THE ROMANTIC STORY OF THE EARLY PIONEERS INTO VIRGINIA, THE CAROLINAS, TENNESSEE, AND KENTUCKY 1740-1790

BY ARCHIBALD HENDERSON, Ph.D., D.C.L.

.

INTRODUCTION

The romantic and thrilling story of the southward and westward migration of successive waves of transplanted European peoples throughout the entire course of the eighteenth century is the history of the growth and evolution of American democracy. Upon the American continent was wrought out, through almost superhuman daring, incredible hardship, and surpassing endurance, the formation of a new society. The European rudely confronted with the pitiless conditions of the wilderness soon discovered that his maintenance, indeed his existence, was conditioned upon his individual efficiency and his resourcefulness in adapting himself to his environment. The very history of the human race, from the age of primitive man to the modern era of enlightened civilization, is traversed in the Old Southwest throughout the course of half a century.

A series of dissolving views thrown upon the screen, picturing the successive episodes in the history of a single family as it wended its way southward along the eastern valleys, resolutely repulsed the sudden attack of the Indians, toiled painfully up the granite slopes of the Appalachians, and pitched down into the transmontane wilderness upon the western waters, would give to the spectator a vivid conception, in miniature, of the westward movement. But certain basic elements in the grand procession, revealed to the sociologist and the economist, would perhaps escape his scrutiny. Back of the individual, back of the family, even, lurk the creative and formative impulses of colonization, expansion, and government. In the recognition of these social and economic tendencies the individual merges into the group; the group into the community; the community into a new society. In this clear perspective of historic development the spectacular hero at first sight seems to diminish; but the mass, the movement, the social force which he epitomizes and interprets, gain in impressiveness and dignity.

As the irresistible tide of migratory peoples swept ever southward and westward, seeking room for expansion and economic independence, a series of frontiers was gradually thrust out toward the wilderness in successive waves of irregular indentation. The true leader in this westward advance, to whom less than his deserts has been accorded by the historian, is the drab and mercenary trader with the Indians. The story of his enterprise and of his adventures begins with the planting of European civilization upon American soil. In the mind of the aborigines he created the passion for the fruits, both good and evil, of the white man's civilization, and he was welcomed by the Indian because he also brought the means for repelling the further advance of that civilization. The trader was of incalculable service to the pioneer in first spying out the land and charting the trackless wilderness. The trail rudely marked by the buffalo became in time the Indian path and the trader's "trace"; and the pioneers upon the westward march, following the line of least resistance, cut out their, roads along these very routes. It is not too much to say that had it not been for the trader—brave, hardy, and adventurous however often crafty, unscrupulous, and immoral—the expansionist movement upon the American continent would have been greatly retarded.

So scattered and ramified were the enterprises and expeditions of the traders with the Indians that the frontier which they established was at best both shifting and unstable. Following far in the wake of these advance agents of the civilization which they so often disgraced, came the cattle-herder or rancher, who took advantage of the extensive pastures and ranges along the uplands and foot-hills to raise immense herds of cattle. Thus was formed what might be called a rancher's frontier, thrust out in advance of the ordinary farming settlements and serving as the first serious barrier against the Indian invasion. The westward movement of population is in this respect a direct advance from the coast. Years before the influx into the Old Southwest of the tides of settlement from the northeast, the more adventurous struck straight westward in the wake of the fur-trader, and here and there erected the cattle-ranges beyond the farming frontier of the piedmont region. The wild horses and cattle which roamed at will through the upland barrens and pea-vine pastures were herded in and driven for sale to the city markets of the East.

The farming frontier of the piedmont plateau constituted the real backbone of western settlement. The pioneering farmers, with the adventurous instincts of the hunter and the explorer, plunged deeper and ever deeper into the wilderness, lured on by the prospect of free and still richer lands in the dim interior. Settlements quickly sprang up in the neighborhood of military posts or rude forts established to serve as safeguards against hostile attack; and trade soon flourished between these

4

settlements and the eastern centers, following the trails of the trader and the more beaten paths of emigration. The bolder settlers who ventured farthest to the westward were held in communication with the East through their dependence upon salt and other necessities of life; and the search for salt-springs in the virgin wilderness was an inevitable consequence of the desire of the pioneer to shake off his dependence upon the coast.

The prime determinative principle of the progressive American civilization of the eighteenth century was the passion for the acquisition of land. The struggle for economic independence developed the germ of American liberty and became the differentiating principle of American character. Here was a vast unappropriated region in the interior of the continent to be had for the seeking, which served as lure and inspiration to the man daring enough to risk his all in its acquisition. It was in accordance with human nature and the principles of political economy that this unknown extent of uninhabited transmontane land, widely renowned for beauty, richness, and fertility, should excite grandiose dreams in the minds of English and Colonials alike. England was said to be "New Land mad and everybody there has his eye fixed on this country." Groups of wealthy or well-to-do individuals organized themselves into land companies for the colonization and exploitation of the West. The pioneer promoter was a powerful creative force in westward expansion; and the activities of the early land companies were decisive factors in the colonization of the wilderness. Whether acting under the authority of a crown grant or proceeding on their own authority, the land companies tended to give stability and permanence to settlements otherwise hazardous and insecure.

The second determinative impulse of the pioneer civilization was wanderlust—the passionately inquisitive instinct of the hunter, the traveler, and the explorer. This restless class of nomadic wanderers was responsible in part for the royal proclamation of 1763, a secondary object of which, according to Edmund Burke, was the limitation of the colonies on the West, as "the charters of many of our old colonies give them, with few exceptions, no bounds to the westward but the South Sea." The Long Hunters, taking their lives in their hands, fared boldly forth to a fabled hunter's paradise in the far-away wilderness, because they were driven by the irresistible desire of a Ponce de Leon or a De Soto to find out the truth about the unknown lands beyond.

But the hunter was not only thrilled with the passion of the chase and of discovery; he was intent also upon collecting the furs and skins of wild animals for lucrative barter and sale in the centers of trade. He was quick to make "tomahawk claims" and to assert "corn rights" as he spied out the rich virgin land for future location and cultivation. Free land and no taxes appealed to the backwoodsman, tired of paying quit-rents to the agents of wealthy lords across the sea. Thus the settler speedily followed in the hunter's wake. In his wake also went many rude and lawless characters of the border, horse thieves and criminals of different sorts, who sought to hide their delinquencies in the merciful liberality of the wilderness. For the most part, however, it was the salutary instinct of the homebuilder—the man with the ax, who made a little clearing in the forest and built there a rude cabin that he bravely defended at all risks against continued assaults—which, in defiance of every restraint, irresistibly thrust westward the thin and jagged line of the frontier. The ax and the surveyor's chain, along with the rifle and the hunting-knife, constituted the armorial bearings of the pioneer. With individual as with corporation, with explorer as with landlord, land-hunger was the master impulse of the era.

The various desires which stimulated and promoted westward expansion were, to be sure, often found in complete conjunction. The trader sought to exploit the Indian for his own advantage, selling him whisky, trinkets, and firearms in return for rich furs and costly peltries; yet he was often a hunter himself and collected great stores of peltries as the result of his solitary and protracted hunting-expeditions. The rancher and the herder sought to exploit the natural vegetation of marsh and upland, the cane-brakes and pea-vines; yet the constantly recurring need for fresh pasturage made him a pioneer also, drove him ever nearer to the mountains, and furnished the economic motive for his westward advance. The small farmer needed the virgin soil of the new region, the alluvial river-bottoms, and the open prairies, for the cultivation of his crops and the grazing of his cattle; yet in the intervals between the tasks of farm life he scoured the wilderness in search of game "and spied out new lands for future settlement".

This restless and nomadic race, says the keenly observant Francis Baily, "delight much to live on the frontiers, where they can enjoy undisturbed, and free from the control of any laws, the blessings which nature has bestowed upon them." Independence of spirit, impatience of restraint, the inquisitive nature, and the nomadic temperament—these are the strains in the American character of the eighteenth century which ultimately blended to create a typical democracy. The rolling of wave after wave of settlement westward across the American continent, with a reversion to primitive conditions along the line of the farthest frontier, and a marked rise in the scale of civilization at each

successive stage of settlement, from the western limit to the
eastern coast, exemplifies from one aspect the history of the
American people during two centuries. This era, constituting the
first stage in our national existence, and productive of a
buoyant national character shaped in democracy upon a free soil,
closed only yesterday with the exhaustion of cultivable free
land, the disappearance of the last frontier, and the recent
death of "Buffalo Bill". The splendid inauguration of the period,
in the region of the Carolinas, Virginia, Tennessee, and
Kentucky, during the second half of the eighteenth century, is
the theme of this story of the pioneers of the Old Southwest.

CONTENTS

8

THE CONQUEST OF THE OLD SOUTHWEST

Chapter I. The Migration of the Peoples

Inhabitants flock in here daily, mostly from Pensilvania and other parts of America, who are over-stocked with people and Mike directly from Europe, they commonly seat themselves towards the West, and have got near the mountains.—Gabriel Johnston, Governor of North Carolina, to the Secretary of the Board of Trade, February 15, 1751.

At the opening of the eighteenth century the tide of population had swept inland to the "fall line", the westward boundary of the established settlements. The actual frontier had been advanced by the more aggressive pioneers to within fifty miles of the Blue Ridge. So rapid was the settlement in North Carolina that in the interval 1717-32 the population quadrupled in numbers. A map of the colonial settlements in 1725 reveals a narrow strip of populated land along the Atlantic coast, of irregular indentation, with occasional isolated nuclei of settlements further in the interior. The civilization thus established continued to maintain a close and unbroken communication with England and the Continent. As long as the settlers, for economic reasons, clung to the coast, they reacted but slowly to the transforming influences of the frontier.. Within a triangle of continental altitude with its apex in New England, bounded on the east by the Atlantic, and on the west by the Appalachian range, lay the settlements, divided into two zones—tidewater and piedmont. As no break occurred in the great mountain system south of the Hudson and Mohawk valleys, the difficulties of cutting a passage through the towering wall of living green long proved an effective obstacle to the crossing of the grim mountain barrier.

In the beginning the settlements gradually extended westward from the coast in irregular outline, the indentations taking form around such natural centers of attraction as areas of fertile soil, frontier posts, mines, salt-springs, and stretches of upland favorable for grazing. After a time a second advance of settlement was begun in New Jersey, Pennsylvania, and Maryland, running in a southwesterly direction along the broad terraces to the east of the Appalachian Range, which in North Carolina lies as far as two hundred and fifty miles from the sea. The Blue Ridge in Virginia and a belt of pine barrens in North Carolina were hindrances to this advance, but did not entirely check it. This second streaming of the population thrust into the long, narrow wedge of the piedmont zone a class of people differing in spirit and in tendency from their more aristocratic and complacent neighbors to the east.

These settlers of the Valley of Virginia and the North Carolina piedmont region—- English, Scotch-Irish, Germans, Scotch, Irish, Welsh, and a few French—were the first pioneers of the Old Southwest. From the joint efforts of two strata of population, geographically, socially, and economically distinct—tidewater and piedmont, Old South and New South—originated and flowered the third and greatest movement of westward expansion, opening with the surmounting of the mountain barrier and ending in the occupation and assumption of the vast medial valley of the continent.

Synchronous with the founding of Jamestown in Virginia, significantly enough, was the first planting of Ulster with the English and Scotch. Emigrants from the Scotch Lowlands, sometimes as many as four thousand a year (1625), continued throughout the century to pour into Ulster. "Those of the North of Ireland . . .," as pungently described in 1679 by the Secretary of State, Leoline Jenkins, to the Duke of Ormond, "are most Scotch and Scotch breed and are the Northern Presbyterians and phanatiques, lusty, able bodied, hardy and stout men, where one may see three or four hundred at every meeting-house on Sunday, and all the North of Ireland is inhabited by these, which is the popular place of all Ireland by far. They are very numerous and greedy after land." During the quarter of a century after the English Revolution of 1688 and the Jacobite uprising in Ireland, which ended in 1691 with the complete submission of Ireland to William and Mary, not less than fifty thousand Scotch, according to Archbishop Synge, settled in Ulster. Until the beginning of the eighteenth century there was no considerable emigration to America; and it was first set up as a consequence of English interference with trade and religion. Repressive measures passed by the English parliament (1665 1699), prohibiting the exportation from Ire land to England and Scotland of cattle, beef, pork, dairy products, *etc.*, and to any country whatever of manufactured wool, had aroused deep resentment among the Scotch-Irish, who had built up a great commerce. This discontent was greatly aggravated by the imposition of religious disabilities upon the Presbyterians, who, in addition to having to pay tithes for the support of the established church, were excluded from all civil and military office (1704), while their ministers were made liable to penalties for celebrating marriages.

This pressure upon a high-spirited people resulted inevitably in an exodus to the New World. The principal ports by which the Ulsterites entered America were Lewes and Newcastle (Delaware), Philadelphia and Boston. The streams of immigration steadily flowed up the Delaware Valley; and by 1720 the Scotch-Irish began to arrive in Bucks County. So rapid was the rate of increase in immigration that the number of arrivals soon mounted from a few hundred to upward of six thousand, in a single year (1729); and within a few years this number was doubled. According to the meticulous Franklin, the proportion increased from a very small element of the population of Pennsylvania in 1700 to one fourth of the whole in 1749, and to one third of the whole (350,000) in 1774. Writing to the Penns in 1724, James Logan, Secretary of the Province, caustically refers to the Ulster settlers on the disputed Maryland line as "these bold and indigent strangers, saying as their excuse when challenged for titles, that we had solicited for colonists and they had come accordingly." The spirit of these defiant squatters is succinctly expressed in their statement to Logan that it "was against the laws of God and nature that so much land should be idle while so many Christians wanted it to work on and to raise their bread."

The rising scale of prices for Pennsylvania lands, changing from ten pounds and two shillings quit-rents per hundred acres in 1719 to fifteen pounds ten shillings per hundred acres with a quit-rent of a halfpenny per acre in 1732, soon turned the eyes of the thrifty Scotch-Irish settlers southward and southwestward. In Maryland in 1738 lands were offered at five pounds sterling per hundred acres. Simultaneously, in the Valley of Virginia free grants of a thousand acres per family were being made. In the North Carolina piedmont region the proprietary, Lord Granville, through his agents was disposing of the most desirable lands to settlers at the rate of three shillings proclamation money for six hundred and forty acres, the unit of land-division; and was also making large free grants on the condition of seating a certain proportion of settlers. "Lord Carteret's land in Carolina," says North Carolina's first American historian, "where the soil was cheap, presented a tempting residence to people of every denomination. Emigrants from the north of Ireland, by the way of Pennsylvania, flocked to that country; and a considerable part of North Carolina . . . is inhabited by those people or their descendants." From 1740 onward, attracted by the rich lure of cheap and even free lands in Virginia and North Carolina, a tide of immigration swept ceaselessly into the valleys of the Shenandoah, the Yadkin, and the Catawba. The immensity of this mobile, drifting mass, which sometimes brought "more than 400 families with horse waggons and cattle" into North Carolina in a single year (1752-3), is attested by the fact that from 1732 to 1754, mainly as the result of the Scotch-Irish inundation, the population of North Carolina more than doubled.

The second important racial stream of population in the settlement of the same region was composed of Germans, attracted to this country from the Palatinate. Lured on by the highly colored stories of the commercial agents for promoting immigration—the "newlanders," who were thoroughly unscrupulous in their methods and extravagant in their representations—a migration from Germany began in the second decade of the eighteenth century and quickly assumed alarming proportions. Although certain of the emigrants were well-to-do, a very great number were "redemptioners" (indentured servants), who in order to pay for their transportation were compelled to pledge themselves to several years of servitude. This economic condition caused the German immigrant, wherever he went, to become a settler of the back country, necessity compelling him to pass by the more expensive lands near the coast.

For well-nigh sixty years the influx of German immigrants of various sects was very great, averaging something like fifteen hundred a year into Pennsylvania alone from 1727 to 1775. Indeed, Pennsylvania, one third of whose population at the beginning of the Revolution was German, early became the great distributing center for the Germans as well as for the Scotch-Irish. Certainly by 1727 Adam Miller and his fellow Germans had established the first permanent white settlement in the Valley of Virginia. By 1732 Jost Heydt, accompanied by sixteen families, came from York, Pennsylvania, and settled on the Opeckon River, in the neighborhood of the present Winchester. There is no longer any doubt that "the portion of the Shenandoah Valley sloping to the north was almost entirely settled by Germans."

It was about the middle of the century that these pioneers of the Old Southwest, the shrewd, industrious, and thrifty Pennsylvania Germans (who came to be generally

11

called "Pennsylvania Dutch" from the incorrect translation of Pennsylvanische Deutsche), began to pour into the piedmont region of North Carolina. In the autumn, after the harvest was in, these ambitious Pennsylvania pioneers would pack up their belongings in wagons and on beasts of burden and head for the southwest, trekking down in the manner of the Boers of South Africa. This movement into the fertile valley lands of the Yadkin and the Catawba continued unabated throughout the entire third quarter of the century. Owing to their unfamiliarity with the English language and the solidarity of their instincts, the German settlers at first had little share in government. But they devotedly played their part in the defense of the exposed settlements and often bore the brunt of Indian attack.

The bravery and hardihood displayed by the itinerant missionaries sent out by the Pennsylvania Synod under the direction of Count Zinzendorf (1742-8), and by the Moravian Church (1748-53), are mirrored in the numerous diaries, written in German, happily preserved to posterity in religious archives of Pennsylvania and North Carolina. These simple, earnest crusaders, animated by pure and unselfish motives, would visit on a single tour of a thousand miles the principal German settlements in Maryland and Virginia (including the present West Virginia). Sometimes they would make an extended circuit through North Carolina, South Carolina, and even Georgia, everywhere bearing witness to the truth of the gospel and seeking to carry the most elemental forms of the Christian religion, preaching and prayer, to the primitive frontiersmen marooned along the outer fringe of white settlements. These arduous journeys in the cause of piety place this type of pioneer of the Old Southwest in alleviating contrast to the often relentless and bloodthirsty figure of the rude borderer.

Noteworthy among these pious pilgrimages is the Virginia journey of Brothers Leonhard Schnell and John Brandmuller (October 12 to December 12, 1749). At the last outpost of civilization, the scattered settlements in Bath and Alleghany counties, these courageous missionaries—feasting the while solely on bear meat, for there was no bread—encountered conditions of almost primitive savagery, of which they give this graphic picture: "Then we came to a house, where we had to lie on bear skins around the fire like the rest . . . . The clothes of the people consist of deer skins, their food of Johnny cakes, deer and bear meat. A kind of white people are found here, who live like savages. Hunting is their chief occupation." Into the valley of the Yadkin in December, 1752, came Bishop Spangenberg and a party of Moravians, accompanied by a surveyor and two guides, for the purpose of locating the one hundred thousand acres of land which had been offered them on easy terms the preceding year by Lord Granville. This journey was remarkable as an illustration of sacrifices willingly made and extreme hardships uncomplainingly endured for the sake of the Moravian brotherhood. In the back country of North Carolina near the Mulberry Fields they found the whole woods full of Cherokee Indians engaged in hunting. A beautiful site for the projected settlement met their delighted gaze at this place; but they soon learned to their regret that it had already been "taken up" by Daniel Boone's future father-in-law, Morgan Bryan.

On October 8, 1753, a party of twelve single men headed by the Rev. Bernhard Adam Grube, set out from Bethlehem, Pennsylvania, to trek down to the new-found haven in the Carolina hinterland—"a corner which the Lord has reserved for the Brethren"—in Anson County. Following for the most part the great highway extending from Philadelphia to the Yadkin, over which passed the great throng sweeping into the back country of North Carolina—through the Valley of Virginia and past Robert Luhny's mill on the James River—they encountered many hardships along the way. Because of their "long wagon," they had much difficulty in crossing one steep mountain; and of this experience Brother Grube, with a touch of modest pride, observes: "People had told us that this hill was most dangerous, and that we would scarcely be able to cross it, for Morgan Bryan, the first to travel this way, had to take the wheels off his wagon and carry it piecemeal to the top, and had been three months on the journey from the Shanidore [Shenandoah] to the Etkin [Yadkin]."

These men were the highest type of the pioneers of the Old Southwest, inspired with the instinct of homemakers in a land where, if idle rumor were to be credited, "the people lived like wild men never hearing of God or His Word." In one hand they bore the implement of agriculture, in the other the book of the gospel of Jesus Christ. True faith shines forth in the simply eloquent words: "We thanked our Saviour that he had so graciously led us hither, and had helped us through all the hard places, for no matter how dangerous it looked, nor how little we saw how we could win through, everything always went better than seemed possible." The promise of a new day—the dawn of the heroic age—rings out in the pious carol of camaraderie at their journey's end:

We hold arrival Lovefeast here,
In Carolina land,
A company of Brethren true,
A little Pilgrim-Band,
Called by the Lord to be of those
Who through the whole world go,
To bear Him witness everywhere,
And nought but Jesus know.

Chapter II. The Cradle of Westward Expansion

In the year 1746 I was up in the country that is now Anson, Orange and Rowan Counties, there was not then above one hundred fighting men there is now at least three thousand for the most part Irish Protestants and Germans and dailey increasing.— Matthew Rowan, President of the North Carolina Council, to the Board of Trade, June 28, 1753.

The conquest of the West is usually attributed to the ready initiative, the stern self-reliance, and the libertarian instinct of the expert backwoodsmen. These bold, nomadic spirits were animated by an unquenchable desire to plunge into the wilderness in search of an El Dorado at the outer verge of civilization, free of taxation, quit-rents, and the law's restraint. They longed to build homes for themselves and their descendants in a limitless, free domain; or else to fare deeper and deeper into the trackless forests in search of adventure. Yet one must not overlook the fact that behind Boone and pioneers of his stamp were men of conspicuous civil and military genius, constructive in purpose and creative in imagination, who devoted their best gifts to actual conquest and colonization. These men of large intellectual mold-themselves surveyors, hunters, and pioneers—were inspired with the larger vision of the expansionist. Whether colonizers, soldiers, or speculators on the grand scale, they sought to open at one great stroke the vast trans-Alleghany regions as a peaceful abode for mankind.

Two distinct classes of society were gradually drawing apart from each other in North Carolina and later in Virginia—the pioneer democracy of the back country and the upland, and the planter aristocracy of the lowland and the tide-water region. From the frontier came the pioneer explorers whose individual enterprise and initiative were such potent factors in the exploitation of the wilderness. From the border counties still in contact with the East came a number of leaders. Thus in the heart of the Old Southwest the two determinative principles already referred to, the inquisitive and the acquisitive instincts, found a fortunate conjunction. The exploratory passion of the pioneer, directed in the interest of commercial enterprise, prepared the way for the great westward migration. The warlike disposition of the hardy backwoodsman, controlled by the exercise of military strategy, accomplished the conquest of the trans-Alleghany country.

Fleeing from the traditional bonds of caste and aristocracy in England and Europe, from economic boycott and civil oppression, from religious persecution and favoritism, many worthy members of society in the first quarter of the eighteenth century sought a haven of refuge in the "Quackerthal" of William Penn, with its trustworthy guarantees of free tolerance in religious faith and the benefits of representative self-government. From East Devonshire in England came George Boone, the grandfather of the great pioneer, and from Wales came Edward Morgan, whose daughter Sarah became the wife of Squire Boone, Daniel's father. These were conspicuous representatives of the Society of Friends, drawn thither by the roseate representations of the great Quaker, William Penn, and by his advanced views on popular government and religious toleration. Hither, too, from Ireland,

14

whither he had gone from Denmark, came Morgan Bryan, settling in Chester County, prior to 1719; and his children, William, Joseph, James, and Morgan, who more than half a century later gave the name to Bryan's Station in Kentucky, were destined to play important roles in the drama of westward migration. In September, 1734, Michael Finley from County Armagh, Ireland, presumably accompanied by his brother Archibald Finley, settled in Bucks County, Pennsylvania. According to the best authorities, Archibald Finley was the father of John Finley, or Findlay as he signed himself, Boone's guide and companion in his exploration of Kentucky in 1769-71. To Pennsylvania also came Mordecai Lincoln, great grandson of Samuel Lincoln, who had emigrated from England to Hingham, Massachusetts, as early as 1637. This Mordecai Lincoln, who in 1720 settled in Chester County, Pennsylvania, the great-great-grandfather of President Lincoln, was the father of Sarah Lincoln, who was wedded to William Boone, and of Abraham Lincoln, who married Anne Boone, William's first cousin. Early settlers in Pennsylvania were members of the Hanks family, one of whom was the maternal grandfather of President Lincoln.

No one race or breed of men can lay claim to exclusive credit for leadership in the hinterland movement and the conquest of the West. Yet one particular stock of people, the Ulster Scots, exhibited with most completeness and picturesqueness a group of conspicuous qualities and attitudes which we now recognize to be typical of the American character as molded by the conditions of frontier life. Cautious, wary, and reserved, these Scots concealed beneath a cool and calculating manner a relentlessness in reasoning power and an intensity of conviction which glowed and burned with almost fanatical ardor. Strict in religious observance and deep in spiritual fervor, they never lost sight of the main chance, combining a shrewd practicality with a wealth of devotion. It has been happily said of them that they kept the Sabbath and everything else they could lay their hands on. In the polity of these men religion and education went hand in hand; and they habitually settled together in communities in order that they might have teachers and preachers of their own choice and persuasion.

In little-known letters and diaries of travelers and itinerant ministers may be found many quaint descriptions and faithful characterizations of the frontier settlers in their habits of life and of the scenes amidst which they labored. In a letter to Edmund Fanning, the cultured Robin Jones, agent of Lord Granville and Attorney-General of North Carolina, summons to view a piquant image of the western border and borderers: "The inhabitants are hospitable in their way, live in plenty and dirt, are stout, of great prowess in manly athletics; and, in private conversation, bold, impertinent, and vain. In the art of war (after the Indian manner) they are well-skilled, are enterprising and fruitful of strategies; and, when in action, are as bold and intrepid as the ancient Romans. The Shawnese acknowledge them their superiors even in their own way of fighting . . . . [The land] may be truly called the land of the mountains, for they are so numerous that when you have reached the summit of one of them, you may see thousands of every shape that the imagination can suggest, seeming to vie with each other which should raise his lofty head to touch the clouds . . . . It seems to me that nature has been wanton in bestowing her blessings on that country."

An excellent pen-picture of educational and cultural conditions in the backwoods of North Carolina, by one of the early settlers in the middle of the century, exhibits in all their barren cheerlessness the hardships and limitations of life in the wilderness. The father of William Few, the narrator, had trekked down from Maryland and settled in Orange County, some miles east of the little hamlet of Hillsborough. "In that country at that time there were no schools, no churches or parsons, or doctors or lawyers; no stores, groceries or taverns, nor do I recollect during the first two years any officer, ecclesiastical, civil or military, except a justice of the peace, a constable and two or three itinerant preachers . . . . These people had few wants, and fewer temptations to vice than those who lived in more refined society, though ignorant. They were more virtuous and more happy . . . . A schoolmaster appeared and offered his services to teach the children of the neighborhood for twenty shillings each per year . . . . In that simple state of society money was but little known; the schoolmaster was the welcome guest of his pupil, fed at the bountiful table and clothed from the domestic loom . . . . In that country at that time there was great scarcity of books."

The journals of itinerant ministers through the Valley of Virginia and the Carolina piedmont zone yield precious mementoes of the people, their longing after the things of the spirit, and their pitiful isolation from the regular preaching of the gospel. These missionaries were true pioneers in this Old Southwest, ardent, dauntless, and heroic—carrying the word into remote places and preaching the gospel beneath the trees of the forest. In his journal (1755-6), the Rev. Hugh McAden, born in Pennsylvania of Scotch-Irish parentage, a graduate of Nassau Hall (1753), makes the unconsciously humorous observation that wherever he found Presbyterians he found people who "seemed highly pleased, and very desirous to hear the word"; whilst elsewhere he found either dissension and defection to Baptist principles, or "no appearance of the life of religion." In the Scotch-Irish Presbyterian settlements in what is now Mecklenburg County, the cradle of American liberty, he found "pretty serious, judicious people" of the stamp of Moses, William, and James Alexander. While traveling in the upper country of South Carolina, he relates with gusto the story of "an old gentleman who said to the Governor of South Carolina, when he was in those parts, in treaty with the Cherokee Indians that 'he had never seen a shirt, been in a fair, heard a sermon, or seen a minister in all his life.' Upon which the governor promised to send him up a minister, that he might hear one sermon before he died." The minister came and preached; and this was all the preaching that had been heard in the upper part of South Carolina before Mr. McAden's visit.

Such, then, were the rude and simple people in the back country of the Old Southwest—the deliberate and self-controlled English, the aggressive, landmongering Scotch-Irish, the buoyant Welsh, the thrifty Germans, the debonair French, the impetuous Irish, and the calculating Scotch. The lives they led were marked by independence of spirit, democratic instincts, and a forthright simplicity. In describing the condition of the English settlers in the backwoods of Virginia, one of their number, Doddridge, says: "Most of the articles were of domestic manufacture. There might have been incidentally a few things brought to the country for sale in a primitive way, but there was no store for general supply. The table furniture usually consisted of wooden vessels, either turned or coopered. Iron forks, tin cups, *etc.*, were articles of rare and delicate luxury. The food was of the most wholesome and primitive kind. The richest meat, the finest butter, and best meal that ever delighted man's palate were here eaten with a relish which health and labor only know. The hospitality of the people was profuse and proverbial."

The circumstances of their lives compelled the pioneers to become self-sustaining. Every immigrant was an adept at many trades. He built his own house, forged his own tools, and made his own clothes. At a very early date rifles were manufactured at the High Shoals of the Yadkin; Squire Boone, Daniel's brother, was an expert gunsmith. The difficulty of securing food for the settlements forced every man to become a hunter and to scour the forest for wild game. Thus the pioneer, through force of sheer necessity, became a dead shot—which stood him in good stead in the days of Indian incursions and bloody retaliatory raids. Primitive in their games, recreations, and amusements, which not infrequently degenerated into contests of savage brutality, the pioneers always set the highest premium upon personal bravery, physical prowess, and skill in manly sports. At all public gatherings, general musters, "vendues" or auctions, and even funerals, whisky flowed with extraordinary freedom. It is worthy of record that among the effects of the Rev. Alexander Craighead, the famous teacher and organizer of Presbyterianism in Mecklenburg and the adjoining region prior to the Revolution, were found a punch bowl and glasses.

The frontier life, with its purifying and hardening influence, bred in these pioneers intellectual traits which constitute the basis of the American character. The single-handed and successful struggle with nature in the tense solitude of the forest developed a spirit of individualism, restive under control. On the other hand, the sense of sharing with others the arduous tasks and dangers of conquering the wilderness gave birth to a strong sense of solidarity arid of human sympathy. With the lure of free lands ever before them, the pioneers developed a restlessness and a nervous energy, blended with a buoyancy of spirit, which are fundamentally American. Yet this same untrammeled freedom occasioned a disregard for law and a defiance of established government which have exhibited themselves throughout the entire course of our history. Initiative, self-reliance, boldness in conception, fertility in resource, readiness in execution, acquisitiveness, inventive genius, appreciation of material advantages—these, shot through with a certain fine idealism, genial human sympathy, and a high romantic strain—are the traits of the American national type as it emerged from the Old Southwest.

CHAPTER III. The Back Country and the Border

Far from the bustle of the world, they live in the most delightful climate, and richest soil imaginable; they are everywhere surrounded with beautiful prospects and sylvan scenes; lofty mountains, transparent streams, falls of water, rich valleys, and majestic woods; the whole interspersed with an infinite variety of flowering shrubs, constitute the landscape surrounding them; they are subject to few diseases; are generally robust; and live in perfect liberty; they are ignorant of want and acquainted with but few vices. Their inexperience of the elegancies of life precludes any regret that they possess not the means of enjoying them, but they possess what many princes would give half their dominion for, health, content, and tranquillity of mind.—Andrew Burnaby: Travels Through North America.

The two streams of Ulstermen, the greater through Philadelphia, the lesser through Charleston, which poured into the Carolinas toward the middle of the century, quickly flooded the back country. The former occupied the Yadkin Valley and tile region to the westward, the latter the Waxhaws and the Anson County region to the northwest. The first settlers were known as the "Pennsylvania Irish," because they had first settled in Pennsylvania after migrating from the north of Ireland; while those who came by way of Charleston were known as the "Scotch-Irish." The former, who had resided in Pennsylvania long enough to be good judges of land, shrewdly made their settlements along the rivers and creeks. The latter, new arrivals and less experienced, settled on thinner land toward the heads of creeks and water courses.

Shortly prior to 1735, Morgan Bryan, his wife Martha, and eight children, together with other families of Quakers from Pennsylvania, settled upon a large tract of land on the northwest side of the Opeckon River near Winchester. A few years later they removed up the Virginia Valley to the Big Lick in the present Roanoke County, intent upon pushing westward to the very outskirts of civilization. In the autumn of 1748, leaving behind his brother William, who had followed him to Roanoke County, Morgan Bryan removed with his family to the Forks of the Yadkin River. The Morgans, with the exception of Richard, who emigrated to Virginia, remained in Pennsylvania, spreading over Philadelphia and Bucks counties; while the Hanks and Lincoln families found homes in Virginia—Mordecai Lincoln's son, John, the great-grandfather of President Lincoln, removing from Berks to the Shenandoah Valley in 1765. On May 1, 1750, Squire Boone, his wife Sarah (Morgan), and their eleven children—a veritable caravan, traveling like the patriarchs of old—started south; and tarried for a space, according to reliable tradition, on Linville Creek in the Virginia Valley. In 1752 they removed to the Forks of the Yadkin, and the following year received from Lord Granville three tracts of land, all situated in Rowan County. About the hamlet of Salisbury, which in 1755 consisted of seven or eight log houses and the court house, there now rapidly gathered a settlement of people marked by strong individuality, sturdy independence, and virile self-reliance. The Boones and the Bryans quickly accommodated themselves to frontier conditions and immediately began to take an active part in the local affairs of the county. Upon the organization of the county court Squire Boone was chosen justice of the peace; and Morgan Bryan was soon appearing as foreman of juries and director in road improvements.

The Great Trading Path, leading from Virginia to the towns of the Catawbas and other Southern Indians, crossed the Yadkin at the Trading Ford and passed a mile southeast of Salisbury. Above Sapona Town near the Trading Ford was Swearing Creek, which, according to constant and picturesque tradition, was the spot where the traders stopped to take a solemn oath never to reveal any unlawful proceedings that might occur during their sojourn among the Indians. In his divertingly satirical "History of the Dividing Line" William Byrd in 1728 thus speaks of this locality: "The Soil is exceedingly rich on both sides the Yadkin, abounding in rank Grass and prodigiously large Trees; and for plenty of Fish, Fowl and Venison, is inferior to No Part of the Northern Continent. There the Traders commonly lie Still for some days, to recruit their Horses' Flesh as well as to recover their own spirits." In this beautiful country happily chosen for settlement by Squire Boone —who erected his cabin on the east side of the Yadkin about a mile and a quarter from Alleman's, now Boone's, Ford—wild game abounded. Buffaloes were encountered in eastern North Carolina by Byrd while running the dividing line; and in the upper country of South Carolina three or four men with their dogs could kill fourteen to twenty buffaloes in a single day." Deer and bears fell an easy prey to the hunter; wild turkeys filled every thicket; the watercourses teemed with beaver, otter, and muskrat, as well as with shad and other delicious fish. Panthers, wildcats, and wolves overran the country; and the veracious Brother Joseph, while near the present Wilkesboro, amusingly records: "The wolves wh. are not like those in Germany, Poland and Lifland (because they fear men and don't easily come near) give us such music of six different cornets the like of wh. I have never heard in my life." So plentiful was the game that the wild deer mingled with the cattle grazing over the wide stretches of luxuriant grass.

In the midst of this sylvan paradise grew up Squire Boone's son, Daniel Boone, a Pennsylvania youth of English stock, Quaker persuasion, and Baptist proclivities. Seen through a glorifying halo after the lapse of a century and three quarters, he rises before us a romantic figure, poised and resolute, simple, benign—as naïve and shy as some wild thing of the primeval forest—five feet eight inches in height, with broad chest and shoulders, dark locks, genial blue eyes arched with fair eyebrows, thin lips and wide mouth, nose of slightly Roman cast, and fair, ruddy countenance. Farming was irksome to this restless, nomadic spirit, who on the slightest excuse would exchange the plow and the grubbing hoe for the long rifle and keen-edged hunting knife. In a single day during the autumn season he would kill four or five deer; or as many bears as would snake from two to three thousand pounds weight of bear-bacon. Fascinated with the forest, he soon found profit as well as pleasure in the pursuit of game; and at excellent fixed prices he sold his peltries, most often at Salisbury, some thirteen miles away, sometimes at the store of the old "Dutchman," George Hartman, on the Yadkin, and occasionally at Bethabara, the Moravian town sixty odd miles distant. Skins were in such demand that they soon came to replace hard money, which was incredibly scarce in the back country, as a medium of exchange. Upon one occasion a caravan from Bethabara hauled three thousand pounds, upon another four thousand pounds, of dressed deerskins to Charleston. So immense was this trade that the year after Boone's arrival at the Forks of Yadkin thirty thousand deerskins were exported from the province of North Carolina. We like to think that the young Daniel Boone was one of that band of whom Brother Joseph, while in camp on the Catawba River (November 12, 1752) wrote: "There are many hunters about here, who live like Indians, they kill many deer selling their hides, and thus live without much work."

In this very class of professional hunters, living like Indians, was thus bred the spirit of individual initiative and strenuous leadership in the great westward expansionist movement of the coming decade. An English traveler gives the following minute picture of the dress and accoutrement of the Carolina backwoodsman.

"Their whole dress is very singular, and not very materially different from that of the Indians; being a hunting shirt, somewhat resembling a waggoner's frock, ornamented with a great many fringes, tied round the middle with a broad belt, much decorated also, in which is fastened a tomahawk, an instrument that serves every purpose of defence and convenience; being a hammer at one side and a sharp hatchet at the other; the shot bag and powderhorn, carved with a variety of whimsical figures and devices, hang from their necks over one shoulder; and on their heads a flapped hat, of a reddish hue, proceeding from the intensely hot beams of the sun.

Sometimes they wear leather breeches, made of Indian dressed elk, or deer skins, but more frequently thin trowsers.

On their legs they have Indian boots, or leggings, made of coarse woollen cloth, that either are wrapped round loosely and tied with garters, or laced upon the outside, and always come better than half-way up the thigh.

On their feet they sometimes wear pumps of their own manufacture, but generally Indian moccossons, of their own construction also, which are made of strong elk's, or buck's skin, dressed soft as for gloves or breeches, drawn together in regular plaits over the toe, and lacing from thence round to the fore part of the middle of the ancle, without a seam in them, yet fitting close to the feet, and are indeed perfectly easy and pliant.

Their hunting, or rifle shirts, they have also died in a variety of colours, some yellow, others red, some brown, and many wear them quite white."

No less unique and bizarre, though less picturesque, was the dress of the women of the region—in particular of Surry County, North Carolina, as described by General William Lenoir:

"The women wore linses [flax] petticoats and 'bedgowns' [like a dressing-sack], and often went without shoes in the summer. Some had bonnets and bedgowns made of calico, but generally of linsey; and some of them wore men's hats. Their hair was commonly clubbed. Once, at a large meeting, I noticed there but two women that had on long gowns. One of these was laced genteelly, and the body of the other was open, and the tail thereof drawn up and tucked in her apron or coat-string."

While Daniel Boone was quietly engaged in the pleasant pursuits of the chase, a vast world-struggle of which he little dreamed was rapidly approaching a crisis. For three quarters of a century this titanic contest between France and England for the interior of the continent had been waged with slowly accumulating force. The irrepressible conflict had been formally inaugurated at Sault *Ste.* Marie in 1671, when Daumont de Saint Lusson, swinging aloft his sword, proclaimed the sovereignty of France over "all countries, rivers, lakes, and streams . . . both those which have been discovered and those which may be discovered hereafter, in all their length and breadth, bounded on the one side by the seas of the North and of the West, and on the other by the South Sea." Just three months later, three hardy pioneers of Virginia, despatched upon their arduous mission by Colonel Abraham Wood in behalf of the English crown, had crossed the Appalachian divide; and upon the banks of a stream whose waters slipped into the Ohio to join the Mississippi and the Gulf of Mexico, had carved the royal insignia upon the blazed trunk of a giant of the forest, the while crying: "Long live Charles the Second, by the grace of God, King of England, Scotland, France, Ireland and Virginia and of the territories thereunto belonging."

La Salle's dream of a New France in the heart of America was blotted out in his tragic death upon the banks of the River Trinity (1687). Yet his mantle was to fall in turn upon the square shoulders of Le Moyne d'Iberville and of his brother—the good, the constant Bienville, who after countless and arduous struggles laid firm the foundations of New Orleans. In the precious treasury of Margry we learn that on reaching Rochelle after his first voyage in 1699 Iberville in these prophetic words voices his faith: "If France does not immediately seize this part of America which is the most beautiful, and establish a colony which is strong enough to resist any which England may have, the English colonies (already considerable in Carolina) will so thrive that in less than a hundred years they will be strong enough to seize all America." But the world-weary Louis Quatorze, nearing his end, quickly tired of that remote and unproductive colony upon the shores of the gulf, so industriously described in Paris as a "terrestrial paradise"; and the "paternal providence of Versailles" willingly yielded place to the monumental speculation of the great financier Antoine Crozat. In this Paris of prolific promotion and amazed credulity, ripe for the colossal scheme of Law, soon to blow to bursting-point the bubble of the Mississippi, the very songs in the street echoed flamboyant, half-satiric panegyrics upon the new Utopia, this Mississippi Land of Cockayne:

It's to-day no contribution
To discuss the Constitution
And the Spanish war's forgot
For a new Utopian spot;
And the very latest phase
Is the Mississippi craze.

Interest in the new colony led to a great development of southwesterly trade from New France. Already the French coureurs de bois were following the water route from the Illinois to South Carolina. Jean Couture, a deserter from the service in New France, journeyed over the Ohio and Tennessee rivers to that colony, and was known as "the greatest Trader and Traveller amongst the Indians for more than Twenty years." In 1714 young Charles Charleville accompanied an old trader from Crozat's colony on the gulf to the great salt-springs on the Cumberland, where a post for trading with the Shawanoes had already been established by the French. But the British were preparing to capture this trade as early as 1694, when Tonti warned Villermont that Carolinians were already established on a branch of the Ohio. Four years later, Nicholson, Governor of Maryland, was urging trade with the Indians of the interior in the effort to displace the French. At an early date the coast colonies began to trade with the Indian tribes of the back country: the Catawbas of the Yadkin Valley; the Cherokees, whose towns were scattered through Tennessee; the Chickasaws, to the westward in northern Mississippi; and the Choctaws farther to the southward. Even before the beginning of the eighteenth century, when the South Carolina settlements extended scarcely twenty miles from the coast, English traders had established posts among the Indian tribes four hundred miles to the west of Charleston. Following the sporadic trading of individuals from Virginia with the inland Indians, the heavily laden caravans of William Byrd were soon regularly passing along the Great Trading Path from Virginia to the towns of the Catawbas and other interior tribes of the Carolinas, delighting the easily captivated fancy and provoking the cupidity of the red men with "Guns, Powder, Shot, Hatchets (which the Indians call Tomahawks), Kettles, red and blue Planes, Duffields, Stroudwater blankets, and some Cutlary Wares, Brass Rings and other Trinkets." In Pennsylvania, George Croghan, the guileful diplomat, who was emissary from the Council to the Ohio Indians (1748), had induced "all-most all the Ingans in the Woods" to declare against the French; and was described by Christopher Gist as a "meer idol among his countrymen, the Irish traders."

Against these advances of British trade and civilization, the French for four decades had artfully struggled, projecting tours of exploration into the vast medial valley of the continent and constructing a chain of forts and trading-posts designed to establish their claims to the country and to hold in check the threatened English thrust from the east. Soon the wilderness ambassador of empire, Celoron de Bienville, was despatched by the far-visioned Galissoniere at Quebec to sow broadcast with ceremonial pomp in the heart of America the seeds of empire, grandiosely graven plates of lasting lead, in defiant yet futile symbol of the asserted sovereignty of France. Thus threatened in the vindication of the rights of their colonial sea-to-sea charters, the English threw off the lethargy with which they had failed to protect their traders, and in grants to the Ohio and Loyal land companies began resolutely to form plans looking to the occupation of the interior. But the French seized the English trading-house at Venango which they converted into a fort; and Virginia's protest, conveyed by a calm and judicious young man, a surveyor, George Washington, availed not to prevent the French from seizing Captain Trent's hastily erected military post at the forks of the Ohio and constructing there a formidable work, named Fort Duquesne. Washington, with his expeditionary force sent to garrison Captain Trent's fort, defeated Jumonville and his small force near Great Meadows

(May, 1754); but soon after he was forced to surrender Fort Necessity to Coulon de Villiers.

The titanic struggle, fittingly precipitated in the backwoods of the Old Southwest, was now on—a struggle in which the resolute pioneers of these backwoods first seriously measured their strength with the French and their copper-hued allies, and learned to surpass the latter in their own mode of warfare. The portentous conflict, destined to assure the eastern half of the continent to Great Britain, is a grim, prophetic harbinger of the mighty movement of the next quarter of a century into the twilight zone of the trans-Alleghany territory:

CHAPTER IV. The Indian War

All met in companies with their wives and children, and set about building little fortifications, to defend themselves from such barbarian and inhuman enemies, whom they concluded would be let loose upon them at pleasure.—The Reverend Hugh McAden—Diary, July, 1755.

Long before the actual outbreak of hostilities powerful forces were gradually converging to produce a clash between the aggressive colonials and the crafty Indians. As the settlers pressed farther westward into the domain of the red men, arrogantly grazing their stock over the cherished hunting-grounds of the Cherokees, the savages, who were already well disposed toward the French, began to manifest a deep indignation against the British colonists because of this callous encroachment upon their territory. During the sporadic forays by scattered bands of Northern Indians upon the Catawbas and other tribes friendly to the pioneers the isolated settlements at the back part of the Carolinas suffered rude and sanguinary onslaughts. In the summer of 1753 a party of northern Indians warring in the French interest made their appearance in Rowan County, which had just been organized, and committed various depredations upon the scattered settlements. To repel these attacks a band of the Catawbas sallied forth, encountered a detached party of the enemy, and slew five of their number. Among the spoils, significantly enough, were silver crucifixes, beads, looking-glasses, tomahawks and other implements of war, all of French manufacture.

Intense rivalry for the good will of the near-by southern tribes existed between Virginia and South Carolina. In strong remonstrance against the alleged attempt of Governor Dinwiddie of Virginia to alienate the Cherokees, Catawbas, Muscogees, and Chickasaws from South Carolina and to attach them to Virginia, Governor Glen of South Carolina made pungent observations to Dinwiddie: "South Carolina is a weak frontier colony, and in case of invasion by the French would be their first object of attack. We have not much to fear, however, while we retain the affection of the Indians around us; but should we forfeit that by any mismanagement on our part, or by the superior address of the French, we are in a miserable situation. The Cherokees alone have several thousand gunmen well acquainted with every inch of the province . . . their country is the key to Carolina." By a treaty concluded at Saluda (November 24, 1753), Glen promised to build the Cherokees a fort near the lower towns, for the protection of themselves and their allies; and the Cherokees on their part agreed to become the subjects of the King of Great Britain and hold their lands under him. This fort, erected this same year on the headwaters of the Savannah, within gunshot distance of the important Indian town of Keowee, was named Fort Prince George. "It is a square," says the founder of the fort (Governor Glen to the Board of Trade, August 26, 1754), "with regular Bastions and four Ravelins it is near Two hundred foot from Salient Angle to Salient Angle and is made of Earth taken out of the Ditch, secured with fachines and well rammed with a banquet on the Inside for the men to stand upon when they fire over, the Ravelins are made of Posts of Lightwood which is very durable, they are ten foot in length sharp pointed three foot and a half in the ground." The dire need for such a fort in the back country was tragically illustrated by the sudden onslaught upon the "House of John Gutry & James Anshers" in York County by a party of sixty French Indians (December 16, 1754), who brutally murdered sixteen of the twenty-one persons present, and carried off as captives the remaining five."

At the outbreak of the French and Indian War in 1754 North Carolina voted twelve thousand pounds for the raising of troops and several thousand pounds additional for the construction of forts—a sum considerably larger than that voted by Virginia. A regiment of two hundred and fifty men was placed under the command of Colonel James Innes of the Cape Fear section; and the ablest officer under him was the young Irishman from the same section, Lieutenant Hugh Waddell. On June 3, 1754, Dinwiddie appointed Innes, his close friend, commander-in-chief of all the forces against the French; and immediately after the disaster at Great Meadows (July, 1754), Innes took command. Within two months the supplies for the North Carolina troops were exhausted; and as Virginia then failed to furnish additional supplies, Colonel Innes had no recourse but to disband his troops and permit them to return home. Appointed governor of Fort Cumberland by General Braddock, he was in command there while Braddock advanced on his disastrous march.

The lesson of Braddock's defeat (July 9, 1755) was memorable in the history of the Old Southwest. Well might Braddock exclaim with his last breath: "Who would have thought it? . . . We shall know better how to deal with them another time." Led on by the reckless and fiery Beaujeu, wearing an Indian gorget about his neck, the savages from the protection of trees and rough defenses, a pre pared ambuscade, poured a galling fire into the compact divisions of the English, whose scarlet coats furnished ideal targets. The obstinacy of the British commanders in refusing to permit their troops to fight Indian fashion was suicidal; for as Herman Alriclis wrote Governor Morris of Pennsylvania (July 22, 1755): " . . . the French and Indians had cast an Intrenchment across the road before our Army which they Discovered not Untill they came Close up to it, from thence and both sides of the road the enemy kept a constant fireing on them, our Army being so confused, they could not fight, and they would not be admitted by the Genl or Sir John St. Clair, to break thro' their Ranks and Take behind trees." Daniel Boone, who went from North Carolina as a wagoner in the company commanded by Edward Brice Dobbs, was on the battle-field; but Dobbs's company at the time was scouting in the woods. When the fierce attack fell upon the baggage a train, Boone succeeded in effecting his escape only by cutting the traces of his team and fleeing on one of the horses. To his dying day Boone continued to censure Braddock's conduct, and reprehended especially his fatal neglect to employ strong flank-guards and a sufficient number of Provincial scouts thoroughly acquainted with the wilderness and all the wiles and strategies of savage warfare.

For a number of months following Braddock's defeat there was a great rush of the frightened people southward. In a letter to Dinwiddie, Washington expresses the apprehension that Augusta, Frederick, and Hampshire County will soon be depopulated, as the whole back country is in motion toward the southern colonies. During this same summer Governor Arthur Dobbs of North Carolina made a tour of exploration through the western part of the colony, seeking a site for a fort to guard the frontier. The frontier company of fifty men which was to garrison the projected fort was placed under the command of Hugh Waddell, now promoted to the rank of captain, though only twenty-one years old. In addition to Waddell's company, armed patrols were required for the protection of the Rowan County frontier; and during the summer Indian alarms were frequent at the Moravian village of Bethabara, whose inhabitants had heard with distress on March 31st of the slaughter of eleven Moravians on the Mahoni and of the ruin of Gnadenhutten. Many of the settlers in the outlying districts of Rowan fled for safety to the refuge of the little village; and frequently every available house, every place of temporary abode was filled with panic stricken refugees. So persistent were the depredations of the Indians and so alarmed were the scattered Rowan settlers by the news of the murders and the destruction of Vaul's Fort in Virginia (June 25, 1756) that at a conference on July 5th the Moravians "decided to protect our houses with palisades, and make them safe before the enemy should in vade our tract or attack us, for if the people were all going to retreat we would be the last left on the frontier and the first point of attack." By July 23d, they had constructed a strong defense for their settlement, afterward called the "Dutch Fort" by the Indians. The principal structure was a stockade, triangular in plan, some three hundred feet on a side, enclosing the principal buildings of the settlement; and the gateway was guarded by an observation tower. The other defense was a stockade embracing eight houses at the mill some distance away, around which a small settlement had sprung up.

During the same year the fort planned by Dobbs was erected upon the site he had chosen—between Third and Fourth creeks; and the commissioners Richard Caswell and Francis Brown, sent out to inspect the fort, made the following picturesque report to the Assembly (December 21, 1756):

"That they had likewise viewed the State of Fort Dobbs, and found it to be a good and Substantial Building of the Dimentions following (that is to say) The Oblong Square fifty three feet by forty, the opposite Angles Twenty four feet and Twenty-Two In Height Twenty four and a half feet as by the Plan annexed Appears, The Thickness of the Walls which are made of Oak Logs regularly Diminished from sixteen Inches to Six, it contains three floors and there may be discharged from each floor at one and the same time about one hundred Musketts the same is beautifully scituated in the fork of Fourth Creek a Branch of the Yadkin River. And that they also found under Command of Cap' Hugh Waddel Forty six Effective men Officers and Soldiers, the said Officers and Soldiers Appearing well and in good Spirits."

As to the erection of a fort on the Tennessee, promised the Cherokees by South Carolina, difficulties between the governor of that province and of Virginia in regard to matters of policy and the proportionate share of expenses made effective cooperation between the two colonies well-nigh impossible. Glen, as we have seen, had resented Dinwiddie's efforts to win the South Carolina Indians over to Virginia's interest. And Dinwiddie had been very indignant when the force promised him by the Indians to aid General Braddock did not arrive, attributing this defection in part to Glen's negotiations for a meeting with the chieftains and in part to the influence of the South Carolina traders, who kept the Indians away by hiring them to go on long hunts for furs and skinns. But there was no such contention between Virginia and North Carolina. Dinwiddie and Dobbs arranged (November 6, 1755) to send a commission from these colonies to treat with the Cherokees and the Catawbas. Virginia sent two commissioners, Colonel William Byrd, third of that name, and Colonel Peter Randolph; while North Carolina sent one, Captain Hugh Waddell. Salisbury, North Carolina, was the place of rendezvous. The treaty with the Catawbas was made at the Catawba Town, presumably the village opposite the mouth of Sugaw Creek, in York County, South Carolina, on February 20-21, 1756; that with the Cherokees on Broad River, North Carolina, March 13-17. As a result of the negotiations and after the receipt of a present of goods, the Catawbas agreed to send forty warriors to aid Virginia within forty days; and the Cherokees, in return for presents and Virginia's promise to contribute her proportion toward the erection of a strong fort, undertook to send four hundred warriors within forty days, "as soon as the said fort shall be built." Virginia and North Carolina thus wisely cooperated to "straighten the path" and "brighten the chain" between the white and the red men, in important treaties which Have largely escaped the attention of historians."

On May 25, 1756, a conference was held at Salisbury between King Heygler and warriors of the Catawba nation on the one side and Chief Justice Henley, doubtless attended by Captain Waddell and his frontier company, on the other. King Heygler, following the lead set by the Cherokees, petitioned the Governor of North Carolina to send the Catawbas some ammunition and to "build us a fort for securing our old men, women and children when we turn out to fight the Enemy on their coming." The chief justice assured the King that the Catawbas would receive a necessary supply of ammunition (one hundred pounds of gunpowder and four hundred pounds of lead were later sent them) and promised to urge with the governor their request to have a fort built as soon as possible. Pathos not unmixed with dry humor tinges the eloquent appeal of good old King Heygler, ever the loyal friend of the whites, at this conference:

"I desire a stop may be put to the selling of strong Liquors by the White people to my people especially near the Indian nation. *If the white people make strong drink, let them. Sell it to one another, or drink it in their own families.* This will avoid a great deal of mischief which otherwise will, happen from my people getting drunk and quarrelling with the White people. I have no strong prisons like you to confine them for it. Our only way is to put them under ground and all these (pointing proudly to his Warriors) will be ready to do that to those who shall deserve it."

In response to this request, the sum of four thousand pounds was appropriated by the North Carolina Assembly for the erection of "a Fort on our western frontier to protect and secure the Catawbas" and for the support of two companies of fifty men each to garrison this and another fort building on the sea coast. The commissioners appointed for the purpose recommended (December 21, 1756) a site for the fort "near the 'Catawba nation"; and on January 20, 1757, Governor Dobbs reported; " We are now building a Fort in the midst of their towns at their own Request." The fort thereupon begun must have stood near the mouth of the South Fork of the

Catawba River, as Dobbs says it was in the "midst" of their towns, which are situated a "few miles north and south of 38 degrees" and might properly be included within a circle of thirty miles radius."

During the succeeding months many depredations were committed by the Indians upon the exposed and scattered settlements. Had it not been for the protection afforded by all these forts, by the militia companies under Alexander Osborne of Rowan and Nathaniel Alexander of Anson, and by a special company of patrollers under Green and Moore, the back settlers who had been so outrageously "pilfered" by the Indians would have "retired from the Frontier into the inner settlements."

CHAPTER V. In Defense of Civilization

We give thanks and praise for the safety and peace vouchsafed us by our Heavenly Father in these times of war. Many of our neighbors, driven hither and yon like deer before wild beasts, came to us for shelter, yet the accustomed order of our congregation life was not disturbed, no, not even by the more than 150 Indians who at sundry times passed by, stopping for a day at a time and being fed by us.—- Wachovia Community Diary, 1757

With commendable energy and expedition Dinwiddie and Dobbs, acting in concert, initiated steps for keeping the engagements conjointly made by the two colonies with the Cherokees and the Catawbas in tile spring and summer of 1756. Enlisting sixty men, "most of them Artificers, with Tools and Provisions," Major Andrew Lewis proceeded in the late spring to Echota in the Cherokee country. Here during the hot summer months they erected the Virginia Fort on the path from Virginia, upon the northern bank of the Little Tennessee, nearly opposite the Indian town of Echota and about twenty-five miles southwest of Knoxville." While the fort was in process of construction, the Cherokees were incessantly tampered with by emissaries from the Nuntewees and the Savannahs in the French interest, and from the French themselves at the Alibamu Fort. So effective were these machinations, supported by extravagant promises and doubtless rich bribes, that the Cherokees soon were outspokenly expressing their desire for a French fort at Great Tellico.

Dinwiddie welcomed the departure from America of Governor Glen of South Carolina, who in his opinion had always acted contrary to the king's interest. From the new governor, William Henry Lyttelton, who arrived in Charleston on June 1, 1756, he hoped to secure effective cooperation in dealing with the Cherokees and the Catawbas. This hope was based upon Lyttelton's recognition, as stated in Dinwiddie's words, of the "Necessity of strict Union between the whole Colonies, with't any of them considering their particular Interest separate from the general Good of the whole." After constructing the fort "with't the least assistance from South Carolina," Major Lewis happened by accident upon a grand council being held in Echota in September. At that time he discovered to his great alarm that the machinations of the French had already produced the greatest imaginable change in the sentiment of the Cherokees. Captain Raymond Demere of the Provincials, with two hundred English troops, had arrived to garrison the fort; but the head men of all the Upper Towns were secretly influenced to agree to write a letter to Captain Demere, ordering him to return immediately to Charleston with all the troops under his command. At the grand council, Atta-kulla-kulla, the great Cherokee chieftain, passionately declared to the head men, who listened approvingly, that "as to the few soldiers of Captain Demere that was there, he would take their Guns, and give them to his young men to hunt with and as to their clothes they would soon be worn out and their skins would be tanned, and be of the same colour as theirs, and that they should live among them as slaves." With impressive dignity Major Lewis rose and earnestly pleaded for the observance of the terms of the treaty solemnly negotiated the preceding March. In response, the crafty and treacherous chieftains desired Lewis to tell the Governor of Virginia that "they had taken up the Hatchet against all

Nations that were Enemies to the English"; but Lewis, an astute student of Indian Psychology, rightly surmised that all their glib professions of friendship and assistance were "only to put a gloss on their knavery." So it proved; for instead of the four hundred warriors promised under the treaty for service in Virginia, the Cherokees sent only seven warriors, accompanied by three women. Al though the Cherokees petitioned Virginia for a number of men to garrison the Virginia fort, Dinwiddie postponed sending the fifty men provided for by the Virginia Assembly until he could reassure himself in regard to the "Behaviour and Intention" of the treacherous Indian allies. This proved to be a prudent decision; for not long after its erection the Virginia fort was destroyed by the Indians.

Whether on account of the dissatisfaction expressed by the Cherokees over the erection of the Virginia fort or because of a recognition of the mistaken policy of garrisoning a work erected by Virginia with troops sent from Charleston, South Carolina immediately proceeded to build another stronghold on the southern bank of the Tennessee at the mouth of Tellico River, some seven miles from the site of the Virginia fort; and here were posted twelve great guns, brought thither at immense labor through the wilderness. To this fort, named Fort Loudoun in honor of Lord Loudoun, then commander-in-chief of all the English forces in America, the Indians allured artisans by donations of land; and during the next three or four years a little settlement sprang up there.

The frontiers of Virginia suffered most from the incursions of hostile Indians during the fourteen months following May 1, 1755. In July, the Rev. Hugh McAden records that he preached in Virginia on a day set apart for fasting and prayer "on account of the wars and many murders, committed by the savage Indians on the back inhabitants." On July 30th a large party of Shawano Indians fell upon the New River settlement and wiped it out of existence. William Ingles was absent at the time of the raid; and Mrs. Ingles, who was captured, afterward effected her escape. The following summer (June 25, 1756), Fort Vaux on the headwaters of the Roanoke, under the command of Captain John Smith, was captured by about one hundred French and Indians, who burnt the fort, killed John Smith junior, John Robinson, John Tracey and John Ingles, wounded four men, and captured twenty-two men, women, and children. Among the captured was the famous Mrs. Mary Ingles, whose husband, John Ingles, was killed; but after being "carried away into Captivity, amongst whom she was barbarously treated," according to her own statement, she finally escaped and returned to Virginia." The frontier continued to be infested by marauding bands of French and Indians; and Dinwiddie gloomily confessed to Dobbs (July 22d): "I apprehend that we shall always be harrass'd with fly'g Parties of these Banditti unless we form an Expedit'n ag'st them, to attack 'em in y'r Towns." Such an expedition, known as the Sandy River Expedition, had been sent out in February to avenge the massacre of the New River settlers; but the enterprise engaged in by about four hundred Virginians and Cherokees under Major Andrew Lewis and Captain Richard Pearis, proved a disastrous failure. Not a single Indian was seen; and the party suffered extraordinary hardships and narrowly escaped starvation.

In conformity with his treaty obligations with the Catawbas, Governor Dobbs commissioned Captain Hugh Waddell to erect the fort promised the Catawbas at the spot chosen by the commissioners near the mouth of the South Fork of the Catawba River. This fort, for which four thousand pounds had been appropriated, was for the most part completed by midsummer, 1757. But owing, it appears, both to the machinations of the French and to the intermeddling of the South Carolina traders, who desired to retain the trade of the Catawbas for that province, Oroloswa, the Catawba King Heygler, sent a "talk" to Governor Lyttelton, requesting that North Carolina desist from the work of construction and that no fort be built except by South Carolina. Accordingly, Governor Dobbs ordered Captain Waddell to discharge the workmen (August 11, 1757); and every effort was made for many months thereafter to conciliate the Catawbas, erstwhile friends of North Carolina. The Catawba fort erected by North Carolina was never fully completed; and several years later South Carolina, having succeeded in alienating the Catawbas from North Carolina, which colony had given them the best possible treatment, built for them a fort at the mouth of Line Creek on the east bank of the Catawba River.

In the spring and summer of 1758 the long expected Indian allies arrived in Virginia, as many as four hundred by May—Cherokees, Catawbas, Tuscaroras, and Nottaways. But Dinwiddie was wholly unable to use them effectively; and in order to provide amusement for them, he directed that they should go "a scalping" with the whites—"a barbarous method of war," frankly acknowledged the governor, "introduced by the French, which we are oblidged to follow in our own defense." Most of the Indian allies discontentedly returned home before the end of the year, but the remainder waited until the next year, to take part in the campaign against Fort Duquesne. Three North Carolina companies, composed of trained soldiers and hardy frontiersmen, went through this campaign under the command of Major Hugh Waddell, the "Washington of North Carolina." Long of limb and broad of chest, powerful, lithe, and active, Waddell was an ideal leader for this arduous service, being fertile in expedient and skilful in the employment of Indian tactics. With true provincial pride Governor Dobbs records that Waddell "had great honor done him, being employed in all reconnoitring parties, and dressed and acted as an Indian; and his sergeant, Rogers, took the only Indian prisoner, who gave Mr. Forbes certain intelligence of the forces in Fort Duquesne, upon which they resolved to proceed." This apparently trivial incident is remarkable, in that it proved to be the decisive factor in a campaign that was about to be abandoned. The information in regard to the state of the garrison at Fort Duquesne, secured from the Indian, for the capture of whom two leading officers had offered a reward of two hundred and fifty pounds, emboldened Forbes to advance rather than to retire. Upon reaching the fort (November 25th), he found it abandoned by the enemy. Sergeant Rogers never received the reward promised by General Forbes and the other English officer; but some time afterward he was compensated by a modest sum from the colony of North Carolina.

A series of unfortunate occurrences, chiefly the fault of the whites, soon resulted in the precipitation of a terrible Indian outbreak. A party of Cherokees, returning home in May, 1758, seized some stray horses on the frontier of Virginia—never dreaming of any wrong, says an old historian, as they saw it frequently done by the whites.

The owners of the horses, hastily forming a party, went in pursuit of the Indians and killed twelve or fourteen of the number. The relatives of the slain Indians, greatly incensed, vowed vengeance upon the whites. Nor was the tactless conduct of Forbes calculated to quiet this resentment; for when Atta-kulla-kulla and nine other chieftains deserted in disgust at the treatment accorded them, they were pursued by Forbes's orders, apprehended and disarmed. This rude treatment, coupled with the brutal and wanton murder of some Cherokee hunters a little earlier, by an irresponsible band of Virginians under Captain Robert Wade, still further aggravated the Indians.

Incited by the French, who had fled to the southward after the fall of Fort Duquesne, parties of bloodthirsty young Indians rushed down upon the settlements and left in their path death and desolation along the frontiers of the Carolinas. On the upper branch of the Yadkin and below the South Yadkin near Fort Dobbs twenty-two whites fell in swift succession before the secret onslaughts of the savages from the lower Cherokee towns. Many of the settlers along the Yadkin fled to the Carolina Fort at Bethabara and the stockade at the mill; and the sheriff of Rowan County suffered siege by the Cherokees, in his home, until rescued by a detachment under Brother Loesch from Bethabara. While many families took refuge in Fort Dobbs, frontiersmen under Captain Morgan Bryan ranged through the mountains to the west of Salisbury and guarded the settlements from the hostile incursions of the savages. So gravely alarmed were the Rowan settlers, compelled by the Indians to desert their planting and crops, that Colonel Harris was despatched post-haste for aid to Cape Fear, arriving there on July 1st. With strenuous energy Captain Waddell, then stationed in the east, rushed two companies of thirty men each to the rescue, sending by water-carriage six swivel guns and ammunition on before him; and these reinforcements brought relief at last to the harassed Rowan frontiers." During the remainder of the year, the borders were kept clear by bold and tireless rangers-under the leadership of expert Indian fighters of the stamp of Grifth Rutherford and Morgan Bryan.

When the Cherokee warriors who had wrought havoc along the North Carolina border in April arrived at their town of Settiquo, they proudly displayed the twenty-two scalps of the slain Rowan settlers. Upon the demand for these scalps by Captain Demere at Fort Loudon and under direction of Atta-kulla-kulla, the Settiquo warriors surrendered eleven of the scalps to Captain Demere who, according to custom in time of peace, buried them. New murders on Pacolet and along the Virginia Path, which occurred shortly afterward, caused gloomy forebodings; and it was plain, says a contemporary gazette, that "the lower Cherokees were not satisfied with the murder of the Rowan settlers, but intended further mischief". On October 1st and again on October 31st, Governor Dobbs received urgent requests from Governor Lyttelton, asking that the North Carolina provincials and militia cooperate to bring him assistance. Although there was no law requiring the troops to march out of the province and the exposed frontiers of North Carolina sorely needed protection, Waddell, now commissioned colonel, assembled a force of five small companies and marched to the aid of Governor Lyttelton. But early in January, 1760, while on the march, Waddell received a letter from Lyttelton, informing him that the assistance was not needed and that a treaty of peace had been negotiated with the Cherokees.

CHAPTER VI. Crushing the Cherokees

Thus ended the Cherokee war, which was among the last humbling strokes given to the expiring power of France in North America.- -Hewatt: An Historical Account of the Rise and Progress of the Colonies of South Carolina and Georgia. 1779.

Governor Lyttelton's treaty of "peace", negotiated with the Cherokees at the close of 1759, was worse than a crime: it was a crass and hideous blunder. His domineering attitude and tyrannical treatment of these Indians had aroused the bitterest animosity. Yet he did not realize that it was no longer safe to trust their word. No sooner did the governor withdraw his army from the borders than the cunning Cherokees, whose passions had been inflamed by what may fairly be called the treacherous conduct of Lyttelton, rushed down with merciless ferocity upon the innocent and defenseless families on the frontier. On February 1, 1760, while a large party (including the family of Patrick Calhoun), numbering in all about one hundred and fifty persons, were removing from the Long Cane settlement to Augusta, they were suddenly attacked by a hundred mounted Cherokees, who slaughtered about fifty of them. After the massacre, many of the children were found helplessly wandering in the woods. One man alone carried to Augusta no less than nine of the pitiful innocents, some horribly mutilated with the tomahawk, others scalped, and all yet alive.

Atrocities defying description continued to be committed, and many people were slain. The Cherokees, under the leadership of Si-lou-ee, or the Young Warrior of Estatoe, the Round O, Tiftoe, and others, were baffled in their persistent efforts to capture Fort Prince George. On February 16th the crafty Oconostota White man to accompany him on a visit to the governor on urgent business, lured the commander, Lieutenant Coytomore, and two attendants to a conference outside the gates. At a preconceived signal a volley of shots rang out; the two attendants were wounded, and Lieutenant Coytomore, riddled with bullets, fell dead. Enraged by this act of treachery, the garrison put to death the Indian hostages within. During the abortive attack upon the fort, Oconostota, unaware of the murder of the hostages, was heard shouting above the din of battle: "Fight strong, and you shall be relieved."

Now began the dark days along the Rowan border, which were so sorely to test human endurance. Many refugees fortified themselves in the different stockades; and Colonel Hugh Waddell with his redoubtable frontier company of Indian-fighters awaited the onslaught of the savages, who were reported to have passed through the mountain defiles and to be approaching along the foot-hills. The story of the investment of Fort Dobbs and the splendidly daring sortie of Waddell and Bailey is best told in Waddell's report to Governor Dobbs (February 29, 1760):

"For several Days I observed a small party of Indians were constantly about the fort, I sent out several parties after them to no purpose, the Evening before last between 8 & 9 o'clock I found by the Dogs making an uncommon Noise there must be a party nigh a Spring which we sometimes use. As my Garrison is but small, and I was apprehensive it might be a scheme to draw out the Garrison, I took our Capt. Bailie who with myself and party made up ten: We had not marched 300 yds. from the fort when we were attacked by at least 60 or 70 Indians. I had given my party Orders not to fire until I gave the word, which they punctually observed: We rec'd the Indians' fire: When I perceived they had almost all fired, I ordered my party to fire which We did not further than 12 steps each loaded with a Bullet and 7 Buck Shot, they had nothing to cover them as they were advancing either to tomahawk us or make us Prisoners: They found the fire very hot from so small a Number which a good deal confused them: I then ordered my party to retreat, as I found the Instant our skirmish began another party had attacked the fort, upon our reinforcing the garrison the Indians were soon repulsed with I am sure a considerable Loss, from what I myself saw as well as those I can confide in they cou'd not have less than 10 or 12 killed and wounded; The next Morning we found a great deal of Blood and one dead whom I suppose they cou'd not find in the night. On my side I had 2 Men wounded one of whom I am afraid will die as he is scalped, the other is in way of Recovery, and one boy killed near the fort whom they durst not advance to scalp. I expected they would have paid me another visit last night, as they attack all Fortifications by Night, but find they did not like their Reception."

Alarmed by Waddell's "offensive-defensive," the Indians abandoned the siege. Robert Campbell, Waddell's ranger, who was scalped in this engagement, subsequently recovered from his wounds and was recompensed by the colony with the sum of twenty pounds.

In addition to the frontier militia, four independent companies were now placed under Waddell's command. Companies of volunteers scoured the woods in search of the lurking Indian foe. These rangers, who were clad in hunting-shirts and buckskin leggings, and who employed Indian tactics in fighting, were captained by such hardy leaders as the veteran Morgan Bryan, the intrepid Griffith Ruthe ford, the German partisan, Martin Phifer (Pfeiffer), and Anthony Hampton, the father of General Wade Hampton. They visited periodically a chain of "forest castles" erected by the settlers—extending all the way from Fort Dobbs and the Moravian fortifications in the Wachau to Samuel Stalnaker's stockade on the Middle Fork of the Holston in Virginia. About the middle of March, thirty volunteer Rowan County rangers encountered a band of forty Cherokees, who fortified themselves in a deserted house near the Catawba River. The famous scout and hunter, John Perkins, assisted by one of his bolder companions, crept up to the house and flung lighted torches upon the roof. One of the Indians, as the smoke became suffocating and the flames burned hotter, exclaimed: "Better for one to die bravely than for all to perish miserably in the flames," and darting forth, dashed rapidly hither and thither, in order to draw as many shots as possible. This act of superb self-sacrifice was successful; and while the rifles of the whites, who riddled the brave Indian with balls, were empty, the other savages made a wild dash for liberty. Seven fell thus under the deadly rain of bullets; but many escaped. Ten of the Indians, all told, lost their scalps, for which the volunteer rangers were subsequently paid one hundred pounds by the colony of North Carolina.

Beaten back from Fort Dobbs, sorely defeated along the Catawba, hotly pursued by the rangers, the Cherokees continued to lurk in the shadows of the dense forests, and at every opportunity to fall suddenly upon way faring settlers and isolated cabins remote from any stronghold. On March 8th William Fish, his son, and Thompson, a companion, were riding along the "trace," in search of provisions for a group of families fortified on the Yadkin, when a flight of arrows hurtled from the cane-brake, and Fish and his son fell dead. Although pierced with two arrows, one in the hip and one clean through his body, Thompson escaped upon his fleet horse; and after a night of ghastly suffering finally reached the Carolina Fort at Bethabara. The good Dr. Bonn, by skilfully extracting the barbed shafts from his body, saved Thompson's life. The pious Moravians rejoiced over the recovery of the brave messenger, whose sensational arrival gave them timely warning of the close proximity of the Indians. While feeding their cattle, settlers were shot from ambush by the lurking foe; and on March 11th, a family barricaded within a burning house, which they were defending with desperate courage, were rescued in the nick of time by the militia. No episode from Fenimore Cooper's Leatherstocking Tales surpasses in melancholy interest Harry Hicks's heroic defense of his little fort on Bean Island Creek. Surrounded by the Indians, Hicks and his family took refuge within the small outer palisade around his humble home. Fighting desperately against terrific odds, he was finally driven from his yard into his log cabin, which he continued to defend with dauntless courage. With every shot he tried to send a redskin to the happy hunting-grounds; and it was only after his powder was exhausted that he fell, fighting to the last, beneath the deadly tomahawk. So impressed were the Indians by his bravery that they spared the life of his wife and his little son; and these were afterward rescued by Waddell when he marched to the Cherokee towns in 1761.

The kindly Moravians had always entertained with generous hospitality the roving bands of Cherokees, who accordingly held them in much esteem and spoke of Bethabara as "the Dutch Fort, where there are good people and much bread." But now, in these dread days, the truth of their daily text was brought forcibly home to the Moravians: "Neither Nehemiah nor his brethren put off their clothes, but prayed as they watched." With Bible in one hand and rifle in the other, the inhabitant of Wachovia sternly marched to religious worship. No Puritan of bleak New England ever showed more resolute courage or greater will to defend the hard-won outpost of civilization than did the pious Moravian of the Wachau. At the new settlement of Bethania on Easter Day, more than four hundred souls, including sixty rangers, listened devoutly to the eloquent sermon of Bishop Spangenberg concerning the way of salvation—the while their arms, stacked without the Gemein Haus, were guarded by the watchful sentinel. On March 14th the watchmen at Bethania with well-aimed shots repelled the Indians, whose hideous yells of baffled rage sounded down the wind like "the howling of a hundred wolves". Religion was no protection against the savages; for three ministers journeying to the present site of Salem were set upon by the red men—one escaping, another suffering capture, and the third, a Baptist, losing his life. A little later word came to Fort Dobbs that John Long and Robert Gillespie of Salisbury had been shot from ambush and scalped—Long having been pierced with eight bullets and Gillespie with seven.

There is one beautiful incident recorded by the Moravians, which has a truly symbolic significance. While the war was at its height, a strong party of Cherokees, who had lost their chief, planned in retaliation to attack Bethabara. "When they went home," sets forth the Moravian Diary, "they said they had been to a great town, where there were a great many people, where the bells rang often, and during the night, time after time, a horn was blown, so that they feared to attack the town and had taken no prisoners." The trumpet of the watchman, announcing the passing of the hour, had convinced the Indians that their plans for attack were discovered; and the regular evening bell, summoning the pious to prayer, rang in the stricken ears of the red men like the clamant call to arms.

Following the retirement from office of Governor Lyttelton, Lieutenant-Governor Bull proceeded to prosecute the war with vigor. On April 1, 1760, twelve hundred men under Colonel Archibald Montgomerie arrived at Charleston, with instructions to strike an immediate blow and to relieve Fort Loudon, then invested by the Cherokees. With his own force, two hundred and ninety-five South Carolina Rangers, forty picked men of the new "levies," and "a good number of guides," Montgomerie moved from Fort Ninety-Six on May 28th. On the first of June, crossing Twelve-Mile River, Montgomerie began the campaign in earnest, devastating and burning every Indian village in the Valley of Keowee, killing and capturing more than a hundred of the Cherokees, and destroying immense stores of corn. Receiving no reply to his summons to the Cherokees of the Middle and Upper Towns to make peace or suffer like treatment, Montgomerie took up his march from Fort Prince George on June 24th, resolved to carry out his threat. On the morning of the 27th, he was drawn into an ambuscade within six miles of Et-chow-ee, eight miles south of the present Franklin, North Carolina, a mile and a half below Smith's Bridge, and was vigorously attacked from dense cover by some six hundred and thirty warriors led by Si-lou-ee. Fighting with Indian tactics, the Provincial Rangers under Patrick Calhoun particularly distinguished themselves; and the bloodcurdling yells of the painted savages were responded to by the wild huzzas of the kilted Highlanders who, waving their Scotch bonnets, impetuously charged the redskins and drove them again and again from their lurking-places. Nevertheless Montgomerie lost from eighty to one hundred in killed and wounded, while the loss of the Indians was supposed to be about half the loss of the whites. Unable to care for his wounded and lacking the means of removing his baggage, Montgomerie silently withdrew his forces. In so doing, he acknowledged defeat, since he was compelled to abandon his original intention of relieving the beleaguered garrison of Fort London.

Captain Demere and his devoted little band, who had been resolutely holding out, were now left to their tragic fate. After the bread was exhausted, the garrison was reduced to the necessity of eating dogs and horses; and the loyal aid of the Indian wives of some of the garrison, who secretly brought them supplies of food daily, enabled them to hold out still longer. Realizing at last the futility of prolonging the hopeless contest, Captain Demere surrendered the fort on August 8, 1760. At daylight the next morning, while on the march to Fort Prince George, the soldiers were set upon by the treacherous Cherokees, who at the first onset killed Captain Demere and twenty-nine others. A humane chieftain, Outassitus, says one of the gazettes of the day, "went around the field calling upon the Indians to desist, and making such representations to them as stopped the further progress and effects of their barbarous and brutal rage," which expressed itself in scalping and hacking off the arms and legs of the defenseless whites. Atta-kulla-kulla, who was friendly to the whites, claimed Captain Stuart, the second officer, as his captive, and bore him away by stealth. After nine days' journey through the wilderness they encountered an advance party under Major Andrew Lewis, sent out by Colonel Byrd, head of a relieving army, to rescue and succor any of the garrison who might effect their escape. Thus Stuart was restored to his friends. This abortive and tragic campaign, in which the victory lay conclusively with the Indians, ended when Byrd disbanded his new levies and Montgomerie sailed from Charleston for the north (August, 1760).

During the remainder of the year, the province of North Carolina remained free of further alarms from the Indians. But the view was generally entertained that one more joint Effort of North Carolina, South Carolina, and Virginia would have to be made in order to humble the Cherokees. At the sessions of the North Carolina Assembly in November and again in December, matters in dispute between Governor Dobbs and the representatives of the people made impossible the passage of a proposed aid bill, providing for five hundred men to cooperate with Virginia and South Carolina. Nevertheless volunteers in large numbers patriotically marched from North Carolina to Charleston and the Congaree (December, 1760, to April, 1761), to enlist in the famous regiment being organized by Colonel Thomas Middleton. On March 31, 1761, Governor Dobbs called together the Assembly to act upon a letter received from General Amherst, outlining a more vigorous plan of campaign appropriate to the succession of a young and vigorous sovereign, George III. An aid bill was passed, providing twenty thousand pounds for men and supplies; and one regiment of five companies of one hundred men each, under the command of Colonel Hugh Waddell, was mustered into service for seven months' duty, beginning May 1, 1761.

On July 7, 1761, Colonel James Grant, detached from the main army in command of a force of twenty-six hundred men, took up his march from Fort Prince George. Attacked on June 10th two miles south of the spot where Montgomerie was engaged the preceding year, Grant's army, after a vigorous engagement lasting several hours, drove off the Indians. The army then proceeded at leisure to lay waste the fifteen towns of the Middle Settlements; and, after this work of systematic devastation was over, returned to Fort Prince George. Peace was concluded in September as the result of this campaign; and in consequence the frontier was pushed seventy miles farther to the west.

Meantime, Colonel Waddell with his force of five hundred North Carolinians had acted in concert with Colonel William Byrd, commanding the Virginia detachment. The combined forces went into camp at Captain Samuel Stalnaker's old place on the Middle Fork of Holston. Because of his deliberately dilatory policy, Byrd was superseded in the command by Colonel Adam Stephen. Marching their forces to the Long Island of Holston, Stephen and Waddell erected there Fort Robinson, in compliance with the instructions of Governor Fauquier, of Virginia. The Cherokees, heartily tired of the war, now sued for peace, which was concluded, independent of the treaty at Charleston, on November 19, 1761.

The successful termination of this campaign had an effect of signal importance in the development of the expansionist spirit. The rich and beautiful lands which fell under the eye of the North Carolina and Virginia pioneers under Waddell, Byrd, and Stephen, lured them irresistibly on to wider casts for fortune and bolder explorations into the unknown, beckoning West.

CHAPTER VII. The Land Companies

It was thought good policy to settle those lands as fast as possible, and that the granting them to men of the first consequence who were likeliest and best able to procure large bodies of people to settle on them was the most probable means of effecting the end proposed.—Acting-Governor Nelson of Virginia to the Earl of Hillsborough: 1770.

Although for several decades the Virginia traders had been passing over the Great Trading Path to the towns of the Cherokees and the Catawbas, it was not until the early years of the eighteenth century that Virginians of imaginative vision directed their eyes to the westward, intent upon crossing the mountains and locating settlements as a firm barrier against the imperialistic designs of France. Acting upon his oft-expressed conviction that once the English settlers had established themselves at the source of the James River "it would not be in the power of the French to dislodge them," Governor Alexander Spotswood in 1716, animated with the spirit of the pioneer, led an expedition of fifty men and a train of pack-horses to the mountains, arduously ascended to the summit of the Blue Ridge, and claimed the country by right of discovery in behalf of his sovereign. In the journal of John Fontaine this vivacious account is given of the historic episode: "I graved my name on a tree by the river side; and the Governor buried a bottle with a paper enclosed on which he writ that he took possession of this place in the name and for King George the First of England. We had a good dinner, and after it we got the men together and loaded all their arms and we drank the King's health in Burgundy and fired a volley, and all the rest of the Royal Family in claret and a volley. We drank the Governor's health and fired another volley."

By this jovial picnic, which the governor afterward commemorated by presenting to each of the gentlemen who accompanied him a golden horseshoe, inscribed with the legend, Sic juvat transcendere montes, Alexander Spotswood anticipated by a third of a century the more ambitious expedition on behalf of France by Celoron de Bienville (see Chapter III), and gave a memorable object-lesson in the true spirit of westward expansion. During the ensuing years it began to dawn upon the minds of men of the stamp of William Byrd and Joshua Gee that there was imperative need for the establishment of a chain of settlements in the trans-Alleghany, a great human wall to withstand the advancing wave of French influence and occupation. By the fifth decade of the century, as we have seen, the Virginia settlers, with their squatter's claims and tomahawk rights, had pushed on to the mountains; and great pressure was brought to bear upon the council to issue grants for vast tracts of land in the uncharted wilderness of the interior.

At this period the English ministry adopted the aggressive policy already mentioned in connection with the French and Indian war, indicative of a determination to contest with France the right to occupy the interior of the continent. This policy had been inaugurated by Virginia with the express purpose of stimulating the adoption of a similar policy by North Carolina and Pennsylvania. Two land companies, organized almost simultaneously, actively promoted the preliminaries necessary to settlement, despatching parties under expert leadership to discover the passes through the mountains and to locate the best land in the trans-Alleghany.

In June, 1749, a great corporation, the Loyal Land Company of Virginia, received a grant of eight hundred thousand acres above the North Carolina line and west of the mountains. Dr. Thomas Walker, an expert surveyor, who in company with several other gentlemen had made a tour of exploration through eastern Tennessee and the Holston region in 1748, was chosen as the agent of this company. Starting from his home in Albemarle County, Virginia, March 6, 1750, accompanied by five stalwart pioneers, Walker made a tour of exploration to the westward, being absent four months and one week. On this journey, which carried the party as far west as the Rockcastle River (May 11th) and as far north as the present Paintsville, Kentucky, they named many natural objects, such as mountains and rivers, after members of the party. Their two principal achievements were the erection of the first house built by white men between the Cumberland Mountains and the Ohio River a feat, however, which led to no important developments; and the discovery of the wonderful gap in the Alleghanies to which Walker gave the name Cumberland, in honor of the ruthless conqueror at Culloden, the "bloody duke."

In 1748 the Ohio Company was organized by Colonel Thomas Lee, president of the Virginia council, and twelve other gentlemen, of Virginia and Maryland. In their petition for five hundred thousand acres, one of the declared objects of the company was "to anticipate the French by taking possession of that country southward of the Lakes to which the French had no right . . . ." By the royal order of May 19, 1749, the company was awarded two hundred thousand acres, free of quit-rent for ten years; and the promise was made of an additional award of the remainder petitioned for, on condition of seating a hundred families upon the original grant and the building and maintaining of a fort. Christopher Gist, summoned from his remote home on the Yadkin in North Carolina, was instructed "to search out and discover the Lands upon the river Ohio & other adjoining branches of the Mississippi down as low as the great Falls thereof." In this journey, which began at Colonel Thomas Cresap's, in Maryland, in October, 1750, and ended at Gist's home on May 18, 1751, Gist visited the Lower Shawnee Town and the Lower Blue Licks, ascended Pilot Knob almost two decades before Find lay and Boone, from the same eminence, "saw with pleasure the beautiful level of Kentucky," intersected Walker's route at two points, and crossed Cumberland Mountain at Pound Gap on the return journey. This was a far more extended journey than Walker's, enabling Gist to explore the fertile valleys of the Muskingum, Scioto, and Miami rivers and to gain a view of the beautiful meadows of Kentucky.

It is eminently significant of the spirit of the age, which was inaugurating an era of land hunger unparalleled in American history, that the first authentic records of the trans-Alleghany were made by surveyors who visited the country as the agents of great land companies. The outbreak of the French and Indian War so soon afterward delayed for a decade and more any important colonization of the West. Indeed, the explorations and findings of Walker and Gist were almost unknown, even to the companies they represented. But the conclusion of peace in 1763, which gave all the region between the mountains and the Mississippi to the British, heralded the true beginning of the westward expansionist movement in the Old Southwest, and inaugurated the constructive leadership of North Carolina in f he occupation and colonization of the imperial domain of Kentucky and the Ohio Valley.

In the middle years of the century many families of Virginia gentry removed to the back country of North Carolina in the fertile region ranging from Williamsborough on the east to Hillsborough on the west. There soon arose in this section of the colony a society marked by intellectual distinction, social graces, and the leisured dignity of the landlord and the large planter. So conspicuous for means, intellect, culture, and refinement were the people of this group, having "abundance of wealth and leisure for enjoyment," that Governor Josiah Martin, in passing through this region some years later, significantly observes: "They have great preeminence, as well with respect to soil and cultivation, as to the manners and condition of the inhabitants, in which last respect the difference is so great that one would be led to think them people of another region." This new wealthy class which was now turning its gaze toward the unoccupied lands along the frontier was "dominated by the democratic ideals of pioneers rather than by the aristocratic tendencies of slave-holding planters." From the cross-fertilization of the ideas of two social groups—-this back-country gentry, of innate qualities of leadership, democratic instincts, economic independence, and expansive tendencies, and the primitive pioneer society of the frontier, frugal in taste, responsive to leadership, bold, ready, and thorough in execution--there evolved the militant American expansion in the Old Southwest.

A conspicuous figure in this society of Virginia emigrants was a young man named Richard Henderson, whose father had removed with his family from Hanover County, Virginia, to Bute, afterward Granville County, North Carolina, in 1742. Educated at home by a private tutor, he began his career as assistant of his father, Samuel Henderson, the High Sheriff of Granville County; and after receiving a law-license, quickly acquired an extensive practice. "Even in the superior courts where oratory and eloquence are as brilliant and powerful as in Westminster hall," records an English acquaintance, "he soon became distinguished and eminent, and his superior genius shone forth with great splendour, and universal applause." This young attorney, wedded to the daughter of an Irish lord, often visited Salisbury on his legal circuit; and here he became well acquainted with Squire Boone, one of the "Worshipfull Justices," and often appeared in suits before him. By his son, the nomadic Daniel Boone, conspicuous already for his solitary wanderings across the dark green mountains to the sun-lit valleys and boundless hunting-grounds beyond, Henderson was from time to time regaled with bizarre and fascinating tales of western exploration; and Boone, in his dark hour of poverty and distress, when he was heavily involved financially, turned for aid to this friend and his partner, who composed the law-firm of Williams and Henderson.

Boone's vivid descriptions of the paradise of the West stimulated Henderson's imaginative mind and attracted his attention to the rich possibilities of unoccupied lands there. While the Board of Trade in drafting the royal proclamation of October 7, 1763, forbade the granting of lands in the vast interior, which was specifically reserved to the Indians, it was clearly not their intention to set permanent western limits to the colonies. The prevailing opinion among the shrewdest men of the period was well expressed by George Washington, who wrote his agent for preempting western lands: "I can never look upon that proclamation in any other light (but I say this between ourselves) than as a temporary expedient to quiet the minds of the Indians." And again in 1767: "It (the proclamation of 1763) must fall, of course, in a few years, especially when those Indians consent to our occupying the lands. Any person, therefore, who neglects the present opportunity of hunting out good lands, and in some measure marking out and distinguishing them for his own, in order to keep others from settling them, will never regain it." Washington had added greatly to his holdings of bounty lands in the West by purchasing at trivial prices the claims of many of the officers and soldiers. Three years later we find him surveying extensive tracts along the Ohio and the Great Kanawha, and, with the vision of the expansionist, making large plans for the establishment of a colony to be seated upon his own lands. Henderson, too, recognized the importance of the great country west of the Appalachians. He agreed with the opinion of Benjamin Franklin, who in 1756 called it "one of the finest in North America for the extreme richness and fertility of the land, the healthy temperature of the air and the mildness of the climate, the plenty of hunting, fishing and fowling, the facility of trade with the Indians and the vast convenience of inland navigation or water carriage." Henderson therefore proceeded to organize a land company for the purpose of acquiring and colonizing a large domain in the West. This partnership, which was entitled Richard Henderson and Company, was composed of a few associates, including Richard Henderson, his uncle and law-partner, John Williams, and, in all probability, their close friends Thomas and Nathaniel Hart of Orange County, North Carolina, immigrants from Hanover County, Virginia.

Seizing the opportunity presented just after the conclusion of peace, the company engaged Daniel Boone as scout and surveyor. He was instructed, while hunting and trapping on his own account, to examine, with respect to their location and fertility, the lands which he visited, and to report his findings upon his return. The secret expedition must have been transacted with commendable circumspection; for although in after years it became common knowledge among his friends that he had acted as the company's agent, Boone himself consistently refrained from betraying the confidence of his employers. Upon a similar mission, Gist had carefully concealed from the suspicious Indians the fact that he carried a compass, which they wittily termed "land stealer"; and Washington likewise imposed secrecy upon his land agent Crawford, insisting that the operation be carried on under the guise of hunting game." The discreet Boone, taciturn and given to keeping his own counsel, in one instance at least deemed it advantageous to communicate the purpose of his mission to some hunters, well known to him, in order to secure the results of their information in regard to the best lands they had encountered in the course of their hunting expedition. Boone came among the hunters, known as the "Blevens connection," at one of their Tennessee station camps on their return from a long hunt in Kentucky, in order, as expressed in the quaint phraseology of the period, to be "informed of the geography and locography of these woods, saying that he was employed to explore them by Henderson & Company." The acquaintance which Boone on this occasion formed with a member of the party, Henry Scaggs, the skilled hunter and explorer, was soon to bear fruit; for shortly afterward Scaggs was employed as prospector by the same land company. In 1764 Scaggs had passed through Cumberland Gap and hunted for the season on the Cumberland; and accordingly the following year, as the agent of Richard Henderson and Company, he was despatched on an extended exploration to the lower Cumberland, fixing his station at the salt lick afterward known as Mansker's Lick.

Richard Henderson thus, it appears, "enlisted the Harts and others in an enterprise which his own genius planned," says Peck, the personal acquaintance and biographer of Boone, "and then encouraged several hunters to explore the country and learn where the best lands lay." Just why Henderson and his associates did not act sooner upon the reports brought back by the hunters—Boone and Scaggs and Callaway, who accompanied Boone in 1764 in the interest of the land company "is not known; but in all probability the fragmentary nature of these reports, however glowing and enthusiastic, was sufficient cause for the delay of five years before the land company, through the agency of Boone and Findlay, succeeded in having a thorough exploration inside of the Kentucky region. Delay was also caused by rival claims to the territory. In the Virginia Gazette of December 1, 1768, Henderson must have read with astonishment not unmixed with dismay that "the Six Nations and all their tributaries have granted a vast extent of country to his majesty, and the Proprietaries of Pennsylvania, and settled an advantageous boundary line between their hunting country and this, and the other colonies to the Southward as far as the Cherokee River, for which they received the most valuable present in goods and dollars that was ever given at any conference since the settlement of America." The news was now bruited about through the colony of North Carolina, that the Cherokees were hot in their resentment because the Northern Indians, the inveterate foes of the Cherokees and the perpetual disputants for the vast Middle Ground of Kentucky, had received at the Treaty of Fort Stanwix, November 5, 1768, an immense compensation from the crown for the territory which they, the Cherokees, claimed from time immemorial. Only three weeks before, John Stuart, Superintendent for Indian Affairs in the Southern Department, had negotiated with the Cherokees the Treaty of Hard Labor, South Carolina (October 14th), by which Governor Tryon's line of 1767, from Reedy River to Tryon Mountain, was continued direct to Colonel Chiswell's mine, the present Wytheville, Virginia, and thence in a straight Brie to the mouth of the Great Kanawha. Thus at the close of the year 1768 the crown through both royal governor and superintendent of Indian affairs acknowledged in fair and open treaty the right of the Cherokees, whose Tennessee villages guarded the gateway, to the valley lands east of the mountain barrier as well as to the dim mid-region of Kentucky. In the very act of negotiating the Treaty of Fort Stanwix, Sir William Johnson privately acknowledged that possession of the trans-Alleghany could be legally obtained only by extinguishing the title of the Cherokees.

These conflicting claims soon led to collisions between the Indians and the company's settlers. In the spring of 1769 occurred one of those incidents in the westward advance which, though slight in itself, was to have a definite bearing upon the course of events in later years. In pursuance of his policy, as agent of the Loyal Land Company, of promoting settlement upon the company's lands, Dr. Thomas Walker, who had visited Powell's Valley the preceding year and come into possession of a very large tract there, simultaneously made proposals to one party of men including the Kirtleys, Captain Rucker, and others, and to another party led by Joseph Martin, trader of Orange County, Virginia, afterward a striking figure in the Old Southwest. The fevered race by these bands of eighteenth-century "sooners" for possession of an early "Cherokee Strip" was won by the latter band, who at once took possession and began to clear; so that when the Kirtleys arrived, Martin coolly handed them "a letter from Dr. Walker that informed them that if we got to the valley first, we were to have 21,000 acres of land, and they were not to interfere with us." Martin and his companions were delighted with the beautiful valley at the base of the Cumberland, quickly "eat and destroyed 23 deer—15 bears—2 buffaloes and a great quantity of turkeys," and entertained gentlemen from Virginia and Maryland who desired to settle more than a hundred families there. The company reckoned, however, without their hosts, the Cherokees, who, fortified by the treaty of Hard Labor (1768) which left this country within the Indian reservation, were determined to drive Martin and his company out. While hunting on the Cumberland River, northwest of Cumberland Gap, Martin and his company were surrounded and disarmed by a party of Cherokees who said they had orders from Cameron, the royal agent, to rob all white men hunting on their lands. When Martin and his party arrived at their station in Powell's Valley, they found it broken up and their goods stolen by the Indians, which left them no recourse but to return to the settlements in Virginia. It was not until six years later that Martin, under the stable influence of the Transylvania Company, was enabled to return to this spot and erect there the station which was to play an integral part in the progress of westward expansion.

Before going on to relate Boone's explorations of Kentucky under the auspices of the land company, it will be convenient to turn back for a moment and give some account of other hunters and explorers who visited that territory between the time of its discovery by Walker and Gist and the advent of Boone.

CHAPTER VIII. The Long Hunters in the Twilight Zone

The long Hunters principally resided in the upper countries of Virginia & North Carolina on New River & Holston River, and when they intended to make a long Hunt (as they calls it) they Collected near the head of Holston near whare Abingdon now stands . . . .—General William Hall.

Before the coming of Walker and Gist in 1750 and 1751 respectively, the region now called Kentucky had, as far as we know, been twice visited by the French, once in 1729 when Chaussegros de Lery and his party visited the Big Bone Lick, and again in the summer of 1749 when the Baron de Longueuil with four hundred and fifty-two Frenchmen and Indians, going to join Bienville in an expedition against "the Cherickees and other Indians lying at the back of Carolina and Georgia," doubtless encamped on the Kentucky shore of the Ohio. Kentucky was also traversed by John Peter Salling with his three adventurous companions in their journey through the Middle West in 1742. But all these early visits, including the memorable expeditions of Walker and Gist, were so little known to the general public that when John Filson wrote the history of Kentucky in 1784 he attributed its discovery to James McBride in 1754. More influential upon the course of westward expansion was an adventure which occurred in 1752, the very year in which the Boones settled down in their Vadkin home.

In the autumn of 1752, a Pennsylvania trader, John Findlay, with three or four companions, descended the Ohio River in a canoe as far as the falls at the present Louisville, Kentucky, and accompanied a party of Shawnees to their town of Es-kip-pa-ki-thi-ki, eleven miles east of what is now Winchester.

This was the site of the "Indian Old Corn Field," the Iroquois name for which ("the place of many fields," or "prairie") was Ken -ta-ke, whence came the name of the state.

Five miles east of this spot, where still may be seen a mound and an ellipse showing the outline of the stockade, is the famous Pilot Knob, from the summit of which the fields surrounding the town lie visible in their smooth expanse. During Findlay's stay at the Indian town other traders from Pennsylvania and Virginia, who reported that they were "on their return from trading with the Cuttawas (Catawbas), a nation who live in the Territories of Carolina," assembled in the vicinity in January, 1753. Here, as the result of disputes arising from their barter, they were set upon and captured by a large party of straggling Indians (Coghnawagas from Montreal) on January 26th; but Findlay and another trader named James Lowry were so fortunate as to escape and return through the wilderness to the Pennsylvania settlements." The incident is of important historic significance; for it was from these traders, who must have followed the Great Warriors' Path to the country of the Catawbas, that Findlay learned of the Ouasioto (Cumberland) Gap traversed by the Indian path. His reminiscences of this gateway to Kentucky, of the site of the old Indian town on Lulbegrud Creek, a tributary of the Red River, and of the Pilot Knobwere sixteen years later to fire Boone to his great tour of exploration in behalf of the Transylvania Company.

During the next two decades, largely because of the hostility of the savage tribes, only a few traders and hunters from the east ranged through the trans-Alleghany. But in 1761, a party of hunters led by a rough frontiersman, Elisha Walden, penetrated into Powell's Valley, followed the Indian trail through Cumberland Gap, explored the Cumberland River, and finally reached the Laurel Mountain where, encountering a party of Indians, they deemed it expedient to return. With Walden went Henry Scaggs, afterward explorer for the Henderson Land Company, William Elevens and Charles Cox, the famous Virginia hunters, one Newman, and some fifteen other stout pioneers. Their itinerary may be traced from the names given to natural objects in honor of members of the party—Walden's Mountain and Walden's Creek, Scaggs' Ridge and Newman's Ridge. Following the peace of 1763, which made travel in this region moderately safe once more, the English proceeded to occupy the territory which they had won. In 1765 George Croghan with a small party, on the way to prepare the inhabitants of the Illinois country for transfer to English sovereignty, visited the Great Bone Licks of Kentucky (May 30th, 31st); and a year later Captain Harry Gordon, chief engineer in the Western Department in North America, visited and minutely described the same licks and the falls. But these, and numerous other water-journeys and expeditions of which no records were kept, though interesting enough in themselves, had little bearing upon the larger phases of westward expansion and colonization.

The decade opening with the year 1765 is the epoch of bold and ever bolder exploration—the more adventurous frontiersmen of the border pushing deep into the wilderness in search of game, lured on by the excitements of the chase and the profit to be derived from the sale of peltries. In midsummer, 1766, Captain James Smith, Joshua Horton, Uriah Stone, William Baker, and a young mulatto slave passed through Cumberland Gap, hunted through the country south of the Cherokee and along the Cumberland and Tennessee rivers, and as Smith reports "found no vestige of any white man." During the same year a party of five hunters from South Carolina, led by Isaac Lindsey, penetrated the Kentucky wilderness to the tributary of the Cumberland, named Stone's River by the former party, for one of their number. Here they encountered two men, who were among the greatest of the western pioneers, and were destined to leave their names in historic association with the early settlement of Kentucky, James Harrod and Michael Stoner, a German, both of whom had descended the Ohio from Fort Pitt. With the year 1769 began those longer and more extended excursions into the interior which were to result in conveying at last to the outside world graphic and detailed information concerning "the wonderful new country of Cantucky." In the late spring of this year Hancock and Richard Taylor (the latter the father of President Zachary Taylor), Abraham Hempinstall, and one Barbour, all true-blue frontiersmen, left their homes in Orange County, Virginia, and hunted extensively in Kentucky and Arkansas. Two of the party traveled through Georgia and East and West Florida; while the other two hunted on the Washita during the winter of 1770-1. Explorations of this type became increasingly hazardous as the animosity of the Indians increased; and from this time onward for a number of years almost all the parties of roving hunters suffered

46

capture or attack by the crafty red men. In this same year Major John McCulloch, living on the south branch of the Potomac, set out accompanied by a white man-servant and a negro, to explore the western country. While passing down the Ohio from Pittsburgh McCulloch was captured by the Indians near the mouth of the Wabash and carried to the present site of Terre Haute, Indiana. Set free after four or five months, he journeyed in company with some French voyageurs first to Natchez and then to New Orleans, whence he made the sea voyage to Philadelphia. Somewhat later, Benjamin Cleveland (afterward famous in the Revolution), attended by four companions, set out from his home on the upper Yadkin to explore the Kentucky wilderness. After passing through Cumberland Gap, they encountered a band of Cherokees who plundered them of everything they had, even to their hats and shoes, and ordered them to leave the Indian hunting-grounds. On their return journey they almost starved, and Cleveland, who was reluctantly forced to kill his faithful little hunting-dog, was wont to declare in after years that it was the sweetest meat he ever ate.

Fired to adventure by the glowing accounts brought back by Uriah Stone, a much more formidable band than any that had hitherto ventured westward—including Uriah Stone as pilot, Gasper Mansker, John Rains, Isaac Bledsoe, and a dozen others—assembled in June, 1769, in the New River region. "Each Man carried two horses," says an early pioneer in describing one of these parties, "traps, a large supply of powder and led, and a small hand vise and bellows, files and screw plate for the purpose of fixing the guns if any of them should get out of fix." Passing through Cumberland Gap, they continued their long journey until they reached Price's Meadow, in the present Wayne County, Kentucky, where they established their encampment. In the course of their explorations, during which they gave various names to prominent natural features, they established their "station camp" on a creek in Sumner County, Tennessee, whence originated the name of Station Camp Creek. Isaac Bledsoe and Gasper Mansker, agreeing to travel from here in opposite directions along a buffalo trace passing near the camp, each succeeded in discovering the famous salt-lick which bears his name—namely Bledsoe's Lick and Mansker's Lick. The flat surrounding the lick, about one hundred acres in extent, discovered by Bledsoe, according to his own statement "was principally Covered with buffelows in every direction—not hundreds but thousands." As he sat on his horse, he shot down two deer in the lick; but the buffaloes blindly trod them in the mud. They did not mind him and his horse except when the wind blew the scent in their nostrils, when they would break and run in droves. Indians often lurked in the neighbourhood of these hunters -plundering their camp, robbing them, and even shooting down one of their number, Robert Crockett, from ambush. After many trials and vicissitudes, which included a journey to the Spanish Natchez and the loss of a great mass of peltries when they were plundered by Piomingo and a war party of Chickasaws, they finilly reached home in the late spring of 1770."

The most notable expedition of this period, projected under the auspices of two bold leaders extraordinarily skilled in woodcraft, Joseph Drake and Henry Scaggs, was organized in the early autumn of 1770. This imposing band of stalwart hunters from the New River and Holston country, some forty in number, garbed in hunting shirts, leggings, and moccasins, with three pack-horses to each man, rifles, ammunition, traps, dogs, blankets, and salt, pushed boldly through Cumberland Gap into the heart of what was later justly named the "Dark and Bloody Ground" (see Chapter XIV)— "not doubting," says an old border chronicler, "that they were to be encountered by Indians, and to subsist on game." From the duration of their absence from home, they received the name of the Long Hunters—the romantic appellation by which they are known in the pioneer history of the Old Southwest. Many natural objects were named by this party—in particular Dick's River, after the noted Cherokee hunter, Captain Dick, who, pleased to be recognized by Charles Scaggs, told the Long Hunters that on *his* river, pointing it out, they would find meat plenty—adding with laconic significance: "Kill it and go home." From the Knob Lick, in Lincoln County, as reported by a member of the party, "they beheld largely over a thousand animals, including buffaloe, elk, bear, and deer, with many wild turkies scattered among them; all quite restless, some playing, and others busily employed in licking the earth . . . . The buffaloe and other animals had so eaten away the soil, that they could, in places, go entirely underground." Upon the return of a detachment to Virginia, fourteen fearless hunters chose to remain; and one day, during the absence of some of the band upon a long exploring trip, the camp was attacked by a straggling party of Indians under Will Emery, a halfbreed Cherokee. Two of the hunters were carried into captivity and never heard of again; a third managed to escape. In embittered commemoration of the plunder of the camp and the destruction of the peltries, they inscribed upon a poplar, which had lost its bark, this emphatic record, followed by their names:

2300 Deer Skins lost Ruination by God

Undismayed by this depressing stroke of fortune, they continued their hunt in the direction of the lick which Bledsoe had discovered the preceding year. Shortly after this discovery, a French voyageur from the Illinois who had hunted and traded in this region for a decade, Timothe de Monbreun, subsequently famous in the history of Tennessee, had visited the lick and killed an enormous number of buffaloes for their tallow and tongues with which he and his companion loaded a keel boat and descended the Cumberland. An early pioneer, William Hall, learned from Isaac Bledsoe that when "the long hunters Crossed the ridge and came down on Bledsoe's Creek in four or five miles of the Lick the Cane had grown up so thick in the woods that they thought they had mistaken the place until they Came to the Lick and saw what had been done . . . . One could walk for several hundred yards a round the Lick and in the lick on buffellows Skuls, & bones and the whole flat round the Lick was bleached with buffellows bones, and they found out the Cause of the Canes growing up so suddenly a few miles around the Lick which was in Consequence of so many buffellows being killed."

This expedition was of genuine importance, opening the eyes of the frontiersmen to the charms of the country and influencing many to settle subsequently in the West, some in Tennessee, some in Kentucky. The elaborate and detailed information brought back by Henry Scaggs exerted an appreciable influence, no doubt, in accelerating the plans of Richard Henderson and Company for the acquisition and colonization of the trans-Alleghany. But while the "Long Hunters" were in

Tennessee and Kentucky the same region was being more extensively and systematically explored by Daniel Boone. To his life, character, and attainments, as the typical "long hunter" and the most influential pioneer we may now turn our particular attention.

CHAPTER IX. Daniel Boone and Wilderness Exploration

Here, where the hand of violence shed the blood of the innocent; where the horrid yells of the savages, and the groans of the distressed, sounded in our ears, we now hear the praises and adorations of our Creator; where wretched wigwams stood, the miserable abodes of savages, we behold the foundations of cities laid, that, in all probability, will equal the glory of the greatest upon earth.—Daniel Boone, 1781.

The wandering life of a border Nimrod in a surpassingly beautiful country teeming with game was the ideal of the frontiersman of the eighteenth century. *As* early as 1728, while running the dividing line between North Carolina and Virginia, William Byrd encountered along the North Carolina frontier the typical figure of the professional hunter: "a famous Woodsman, call'd Epaphroditus Bainton. This Forester Spends all his time in ranging the Woods, and is said to make great Havock among the Deer, and other Inhabitants of the Forest, not much wilder than himself." By the middle of the century, as he was threading his way through the Carolina piedmont zone, the hunter's paradise of the Yadkin and Catawba country, Bishop Spangenberg found ranging there many hunters, living like Indians, who killed thousands of deer each year and sold the skins in the local markets or to the fur-traders from Virginia whose heavy pack-trains with their tinkling bells constantly traversed the course of the Great Trading Path. The superlative skill of one of these hunters, both as woodsman and marksman, was proverbial along the border. The name of Daniel Boone became synonymous with expert huntsmanship and almost uncanny wisdom in forest lore. The bottoms of the creek near the Boone home, three miles west of present Mocksville, contained a heavy growth of beech, which dropped large quantities of its rich nuts or mast, greatly relished by bears; and this creek received its name, Bear Creek, because Daniel and his father killed in its rich bottoms ninety-nine bears in a single hunting-season. After living for a time with his young wife, Rebecca Bryan, in a cabin in his father's yard, Daniel built a home of his own upon a tract of land, purchased from his father on October 12, 1759, and lying on Sugar Tree, a tributary of Dutchman's Creek. Here he dwelt for the next five years, with the exception of the period of his temporary removal to Virginia during the terrible era of the Indian war. Most of his time during the autumn and winter, when he was not engaged in wagoning or farming, he spent in long hunting-journeys into the mountains to the west and northwest. During the hunting-season of 1760 he struck deeper than ever before into the western mountain region and encamped in a natural rocky shelter amidst fine hunting-grounds, in what is now Washington County in east Tennessee. Of the scores of inscriptions commemorative of his hunting-feats, which Boone with pardonable pride was accustomed throughout his life time to engrave with his hunting-knife upon trees and rocks, the earliest known is found upon a leaning beech tree, only recently fallen, near his camp and the creek which since that day has borne his name. This is a characteristic and enduring record in the history of American exploration

    D. Boon
CillED A. *Bar* On
      Tree

in The
yEAR
1760

Late in the summer of the following year Boone marched under the command of the noted Indian-fighter of the border, Colonel Hugh Waddell, in his campaign against the Cherokees. From the lips of Waddell, who was outspoken in his condemnation of Byrd's futile delays in road-cutting and fort-building, Boone learned the true secret of success in Indian warfare, which was lost upon Braddock, Forbes, and later St. Clair: that the art of defeating red men was to deal them a sudden and unexpected blow, before they had time either to learn the strength of the force employed against them or to lay with subtle craft their artful ambuscade.

In the late autumn of 1761, Daniel Boone and Nathaniel Gist, the son of Washington's famous guide, who were both serving under Waddell, temporarily detached themselves from his command and led a small party on a "long hunt" in the Valley of the Holston, While encamping near the site of Black's Fort, subsequently built, they were violently assailed by a pack of fierce wolves which they had considerable difficulty in beating off; and from this incident the locality became known as Wolf Hills (now Abingdon, Virginia).

From this time forward Boone's roving instincts had full sway. For many months each year he threaded his way through that marvelously beautiful country of western North Carolina felicitously described as the Switzerland of America. Boone's love of solitude and the murmuring forest was surely inspired by the phenomenal beauties of the country' through which he roamed at will. Blowing Rock on one arm of a great horseshoe of mountains and Tryon Mountain upon the other arm, overlooked an enormous, primeval bowl, studded by a thousand emerald-clad eminences. There was the Pilot Mountain, the towering and isolated pile which from time immemorial had served the aborigines as a guide in their forest wanderings; there was the dizzy height of the Roan on the border; there was Mt. Mitchell, portentous in its grandeur, the tallest peak on the continent east of the Rockies; and there was the Grandfather, the oldest mountain on earth according to geologists, of which it has been written:

Oldest of all terrestrial things—still holding
Thy wrinkled forehead high;
Whose every scam, earth's history enfolding,
Grim science doth defy!

Thou caught'st the far faint ray from Sirius rising,
When through space first was hurled
The primal gloom of ancient voids surprising,
This atom, called the World!

What more gratifying to the eye of the wanderer than the luxuriant vegetation and lavish profusion of the gorgeous flowers upon the mountain slopes, radiant rhododendron, rosebay, and laurel, and the azalea rising like flame; or the rare

51

beauties of the water—the cataract of Linville, taking its shimmering leap into the gorge, and that romantic river poetically celebrated in the lines:

Swannanoa, nymph of beauty,
I would woo thee in my rhyme,
Wildest, brightest, loveliest river
Of our sunny Southern clime.
    * * *
Gone forever from the borders
But immortal in thy name,
Are the Red Men of the forest
Be thou keeper of their fame!
Paler races dwell beside thee,
Celt and Saxon till thy lands
Wedding use unto thy beauty
Linking over thee their hands.

The long rambling excursions which Boone made through western North Carolina and eastern Tennessee enabled him to explore every nook and corner of the rugged and beautiful mountain region. Among the companions and contemporaries with whom he hunted and explored the country were his little son James and his brother Jesse; the Linville who gave the name to the beautiful falls; Julius Cæsar Dugger, whose rock house stood near the head of Elk Creek; and Nathaniel Gist, who described for him the lofty gateway to Kentucky, through which Christopher Gist had passed in 1751. Boone had already heard of this gateway, from Findlay, and it was one of the secret and cherished ambitions of his life to scale the mountain wall of the Appalachians and to reach that high portal of the Cumberland which beckoned to the mysterious new Eden beyond. Although hunting was an endless delight to Boone he was haunted in the midst of this pleasure, as was Kipling's Explorer, by the lure of the undiscovered:

Till a voice as bad as conscience, rang interminable changes On one everlasting whisper day and night repeated—so: 'Something hidden. Go and find it. Go and look behind the ranges-- 'Something lost behind the ranges. Lost and waiting for you. Go.'

Of Boone's preliminary explorations for the land company known as Richard Henderson and Company, an account has already been given; and the delay in following them up has been touched on and in part explained. Meanwhile Boone transferred his efforts for a time to another field. Toward the close of the summer of 1765 a party consisting of Major John Field, William Hill, one Slaughter, and two others, all from Culpeper County, Virginia, visited Boone and induced him to accompany them on the "long Journey" to Florida, whither they were attracted by the liberal offer of Colonel James Grant, governor of the eastern section, the Florida of to-day. On this long and arduous expedition they suffered many hardships and endured many privations, found little game, and on one occasion narrowly escaped starvation. They explored Florida from St. Augustine to Pensacola; and Boone, who

52

relished fresh scenes and a new environment, purchased a house and lot in Pensacola in anticipation of removal thither. But upon his return home, finding his wife unwilling to go, Boone once more turned his eager eye toward the West, that mysterious and alluring region beyond the great range, the fabled paradise of Kentucky.

The following year four young men from the Yadkin, Benjamin Cutbird, John Stewart (Boone's brother-in-law who afterwards accompanied him to Kentucky), John Baker, and James Ward made a remarkable journey to the westward, crossing the Appalachian mountain chain over some unknown route, and finally reaching the Mississippi. The significance of the journey, in its bearing upon westward expansion, inheres in the fact that while for more than half a century the English traders from South Carolina had been winning their way to the Mississippi along the lower routes and Indian trails, this was the first party from either of the Carolinas, as far as is known, that ever reached the Mississippi by crossing the great mountain barrier. When Cutbird, a superb woodsman and veritable Leather stocking, narrated to Boone the story of his adventures, it only confirmed Boone in his determination to find the passage through the mountain chain leading to the Mesopotamia of Kentucky.

Such an enterprise was attended by terrible dangers. During 1766 and 1767 the steady encroachments of the white settlers upon the ancestral domain which the Indians reserved for their imperial hunting-preserve aroused bitter feelings of resentment among the red men. Bloody reprisal was often the sequel to such encroachment. The vast region of Tennessee and the trans-Alleghany was a twilight zone, through which the savages roamed at will. From time to time war parties of northern Indians, the inveterate foes of the Cherokees, scouted through this no-man's land and even penetrated into the western region of North Carolina, committing murders and depredations upon the Cherokees and the whites indiscriminately. During the summer of 1766, while Boone's friend and close connection, Captain William Linville, his son John, and another young man, named John Williams, were in camp some ten miles below Linville Falls, they were unexpectedly fired upon by a hostile band of Northern Indians, and before they had time to fire a shot, a second volley killed both the Linvilles and severely wounded Williams, who after extraordinary sufferings finally reached the settlements." In May, 1767, four traders and a half-breed child of one of them were killed in the Cherokee country. In the summer of this year Governor William Tryon of North Carolina laid out the boundary line of the Cherokees, and upon his return issued a proclamation forbidding any purchase of land from the Indians and any issuance of grants for land within one mile of the boundary line. Despite this wise precaution, seven North Carolina hunters who during the following September had lawlessly ventured into the mountain region some sixty miles beyond the boundary were fired upon, and several of them killed, by the resentful Cherokees Undismayed by these signs of impending danger, undeterred even by the tragic fate of the Linvilles, Daniel Boone, with the determination of the indomitable pioneer, never dreamed of relinquishing his long-cherished design. Discouraged by the steady disappearance of game under the ruthless attack of innumerable hunters, Boone continued to direct his thoughts toward the project of exploring the fair region of Kentucky. The adventurous

William Hill, to whom Boone communicated his purpose, readily consented to go with him; and in the autumn of 1768 Boone and Hill, accompanied, it is believed, by Squire Boone, Daniel's brother, set forth upon their almost inconceivably hazardous expedition. They crossed the Blue Ridge and the Alleghanies, the Holston and Clinch rivers near their sources, and finally reached the head waters of the West Fork of the Big Sand. Surmising from its course that this stream must flow into the Ohio, they pushed on a hundred miles to the westward and finally, by following a buffalo path, reached a salt-spring in what is now Floyd County, in the extreme eastern section of Kentucky. Here Boone beheld great droves of buffalo that visited the salt-spring to drink the water or lick the brackish soil. After spending the winter in hunting and trapping, the Boones and Hill, discouraged by the forbidding aspect of the hill-country which with its dense growth of laurel was exceedingly difficult to penetrate, abandoned all hope of finding Kentucky by this route and wended their arduous way back to the Yadkin.

The account of Boone's subsequent accomplishment of his purpose must be postponed to the next chapter.

CHAPTER X. Daniel Boone in Kentucky

He felt very much as Columbus did, gazing from his caravel on San Salvador; as Cortes, looking down, from the crest of Ahualco, on the Valley of Mexico; or Vasco Nunez, standing alone on the peak of Darien, and stretching his eyes over the hitherto undiscovered waters of the Pacific.——William Gilmore Simms: Views and Reviews.

A chance acquaintance formed by Daniel Boone, during the French and Indian War, with the Irish lover of adventure, John Findlay, was the origin of Boone's cherished longing to reach the El Dorado of the West. In this slight incident we may discern the initial inspiration for the epochal movement of westward expansion. Findlay was a trader and horse peddler, who had early migrated to Carlisle, Pennsylvania. He had been licensed a trader with the Indians in 1747. During the same year he was married to Elizabeth Harris, daughter of John Harris, the Indian-trader at Harris's Ferry on the Susquehanna River, after whom Harrisburg was named. During the next eight years Findlay carried on his business of trading in the interior. Upon the opening of the French and Indian War he was probably among "the young men about Paxtang who enlisted immediately," and served as a waggoner in Braddock's expedition. Over the campfires, during the ensuing campaign in 1765, young Boone was an eager listener to Findlay's stirring narrative of his adventures in the Ohio Valley and on the wonderfully beautiful levels of Kentucky in 1752. The fancies aroused in his brooding mind by Findlay's moving recital and his description of an ancient passage through the Ouasioto or Cumberland Gap and along the course of the Warrior's Path, inspired him with an irrepressible longing to reach that alluring promised land which was the perfect realization of the hunter's paradise.

Thirteen years later, while engaged in selling pins, needles, thread, and Irish linens in the Yadkin country, Findlay learned from the Pennsylvania settlers at Salisbury or at the Forks of the Yadkin of Boone's removal to the waters of the upper Yadkin. At Boone's rustic home, in the winter of 1768-9, Findlay visited his old comrade-in-arms of Braddock's campaign. On learning of Boone's failure during the preceding year to reach the Kentucky levels by way of the inhospitable Sandy region, Findlay again described to him the route through the Ouasioto Gap traversed sixteen years before by Pennsylvania traders in their traffic with the Catawbas. Boone, as we have seen, knew that Christopher Gist, who had formerly lived near him on the upper Yadkin, had found some passage through the lofty mountain defiles; but he had never been able to discover the passage. Findlay's renewed descriptions of the immense herds of buffaloes he had seen in Kentucky, the great salt-licks where they congregated, the abundance of bears, deer, and elk with which the country teemed, the innumerable flocks of wild turkeys, geese, and ducks, aroused in Boone the hunter's passion for the chase; while the beauty of the lands, as mirrored in the vivid fancy of the Irishman, inspired him with a new longing to explore the famous country which had, as John Filson records, "greatly engaged Mr. Findlay's attention."

In the comprehensive designs of Henderson, now a judge, for securing a "graphic report of the trans-Alleghany region in behalf of his land company", Boone divined the means of securing the financial backing for an expedition of considerable size and ample equipment. In numerous suits for debt, aggregating hundreds of dollars, which had been instituted against Boone by some of the leading citizens of Rowan, Williams and Henderson had acted as Boone's attorneys. In order to collect their legal fees, they likewise brought suit against Boone; but not wishing to press the action against the kindly scout who had hitherto acted as their agent in western exploration, they continued the litigation from court to court, in lieu of certain "conditions performed" on behalf of Boone, during his unbroken absence, by his attorney in this suit, Alexander Martin. Summoned to appear in 1769 at the March term of court at Salisbury, Boone seized upon the occasion to lay before Judge Henderson the designs for a renewed and extended exploration of Kentucky suggested by the golden opportunity of securing the services of Findlay as guide. Shortly after March 6th, when Judge Henderson reached Salisbury, the conference, doubtless attended by John Stewart, Boone's brother-in-law, John Findlay, and Boone, who were all present at this term of court, must have been held, for the purpose of devising ways and means for the expedition. Peck, the only reliable contemporary biographer of the pioneer, who derived many facts from Boone himself and his intimate acquaintances, draws the conclusion (1847): "Daniel Boone was engaged as the master spirit of this exploration, because in his judgment and fidelity entire confidence could be reposed . . . . He was known to Henderson and encouraged by him to make the exploration, and to examine particularly the whole country south of the Kentucky—or as then called the Louisa River." As confidential agent of the land company, Boone carried with him letters and instructions for his guidance upon this extended tour of exploration."

On May 1, 1769, with Findlay as guide, and accompanied by four of his neighbors, John Stewart, a skilled woodsman, Joseph Holden, James Mooney, and William Cooley, Boone left his "peaceable habitation" on the upper Yadkin and began his historic journey "in quest of the country of Kentucky." Already heavily burdened with debts, Boone must have incurred considerable further financial obligations to Judge Henderson and Colonel Williams, acting for the land company, in order to obtain the large amount of supplies requisite for so prolonged an expedition. Each of the adventurers rode a good horse of strength and endurance; and behind him were securely strapped the blanket, ammunition, salt, and cooking-utensils so indispensable for a long sojourn in the wilderness. In Powell's Valley they doubtless encountered the party led thither by Joseph Martin (see Chapter VII), and there fell into the "Hunter's Trail" commented on in a letter written by Martin only a fortnight before the passing of Boone's cavalcade. Crossing the mountain at the Ouasioto Gap, they made their first "station camp" in Kentucky on the creek, still named after that circumstance, on the Red Lick Fork. After a preliminary journey for the purpose of locating the spot, Findlay led the party to his old trading-camp at Es-kip-pa-ki-thi-ki, where then (June 7, 1769) remained but charred embers of the Indian huts, with some of the stockading and the gate-posts still standing. In Boone's own words, he and Findlay at once "proceeded to take a more thorough survey of the country;" and during the autumn and early winter, encountering on every hand apparently inexhaustible stocks of wild game and noting the ever-changing beauties of the country, the various members of the party made many hunting and exploring journeys from their "station camp" as base. On December 22, 1769, while engaged in a hunt, Boone and Stewart were surprised and captured by a large party of Shawanoes, led by Captain Will, who were returning from the autumn hunt on Green River to their villages north of the Ohio. Boone and Stewart were forced to pilot the Indians to their main camp, where the savages, after robbing them of all their peltries and supplies and leaving them inferior guns and little ammunition, set off to the northward. They left, on parting, this menacing admonition to the white intruders: "Now, brothers, go home and stay there. Don't come here any more, for this is the Indians' hunting-ground, and all the animals, skins, and furs are ours. If you are so foolish as to venture here again, you may be sure the wasps and yellow jackets will sting you severely."

Chagrined particularly by the loss of the horses, Boone and Stewart for two days pursued the Indians in hot haste. Finally approaching the Indians' camp by stealth in the dead of night, they secured two of the horses, upon which they fled at top speed. In turn they were immediately pursued by a detachment of the Indians, mounted upon their fleetest horses; and suffered the humiliation of recapture two days later. Indulging in wild hilarity over the capture of the crestfallen whites, the Indians took a bell from one of the horses and, fastening it about Boone's neck, compelled him under the threat of brandished tomahawks to caper about and jingle the bell, jeering at him the while with the derisive query, uttered in broken English: "Steal horse, eh?" With as good grace as they could summon—wry smiles at best—Boone and Stewart patiently endured these humiliations, following the Indians as captives. Some days later (about January 4, 1770), while the vigilance of the Indians was momentarily relaxed, the captives suddenly plunged into a dense canebrake and in the subsequent confusion succeeded in effecting their escape. Finding their camp deserted upon their return, Boone and Stewart hastened on and finally overtook their companions. Here Boone was both surprised and delighted to encounter his brother Squire, loaded down with supplies. Having heard nothing from Boone, the partners of the land company had surmised that he and his party must have run short of ammunition, flour, salt, and other things sorely needed in the wilderness; and because of their desire that the party should remain, in order to make an exhaustive exploration of the country, Squire Boone had been sent to him with supplies. Findlay, Holden, Mooney, and Cooley returned to the settlements; but Stewart, Squire Boone, and Alexander Neely, who had accompanied Squire, threw in their lot with the intrepid Daniel, and fared forth once more to the stirring and bracing adventures of the Kentucky wilderness. In Daniel Boone's own words, he expected "from the furs and peltries they had an opportunity of taking . . . to recruit his shattered circumstances; discharge the debts he had contracted by the adventure; and shortly return under better auspices, to settle the newly discovered country."

Boone and his party now stationed themselves near the mouth of the Red River, and soon provided themselves, against the hard. ships of the long winter, with jerk, bear's oil, buffalo tallow, dried buffalo tongues, fresh meat, and marrow-bones as food, and buffalo robes and bearskins as shelter from the inclement weather. Neely had brought with him, to while away dull hours, a copy of "Gulliver's Travels"; and in describing Neely's successful hunt for buffalo one day, Boone in after years amusingly deposed: "In the year 1770 I encamped on Red River with five other men, and we had with us for our amusement the History of Samuel Gulliver's Travels, wherein he gave an account of his young master, Glumdelick, careing him on market day for a show to a town called Lulbegrud. A young man of our company called Alexander Neely came to camp and told us he had been that day to Lulbegrud, and had killed two Brobdignags in their capital." Far from unlettered were pioneers who indulged together in such literary chat and gave to the near-by creek the name (after Dean Swift's Lorbrugrud) of Lulbegrud which name, first seen on Filson's map of Kentucky (1784), it bears to this day. From one of his long, solitary hunts Stewart never returned; and it was not until five years later, while cutting out the Transylvania Trail, that Boone and his companions discovered, near the old crossing at Rockcastle, Stewart's remains in a standing hollow sycamore. The wilderness never gave up its tragic secret.

The close of the winter and most of the spring were passed by the Boones, after Neely's return to the settlements, in exploration, hunting, and trapping beaver and otter, in which sport Daniel particularly excelled. Owing to the drain upon their ammunition, Squire was at length compelled to return to the settlements for supplies; and Daniel, who remained alone in the wilderness to complete his explorations for the land company, must often have shared the feelings of Balboa as, from lofty knob or towering ridge, he gazed over the waste of forest which spread from the dim out lines of the Alleghanies to the distant waters of the Mississippi. He now proceeded to make those remarkable solitary explorations of Kentucky which have given him immortality— through the valley of the Kentucky and the Licking, and along the "Belle Riviere" (Ohio) as low as the falls. He visited the Big Bone Lick and examined the wonderful fossil remains of the mammoth found there. Along the great buffalo roads, worn several feet below the surface of the ground, which led to the Blue Licks, he saw with amazement and delight thousands of huge shaggy buffalo gamboling, bellowing, and making the earth rumble beneath the trampling of their hooves. One day, while upon a cliff near the junction of the Kentucky and Dick's Rivers, he suddenly found himself hemmed in by a party of Indians. Seizing his only chance of escape, he leaped into the top of a maple tree growing beneath the cliffs and, sliding to safety full sixty feet below, made his escape, pursued by the sound of a chorus of guttural "Ughs" from the dumbfounded savages.

Finally making his way back to the old camp, Daniel was rejoined there by Squire on July 27, 1770. During the succeeding months, much of their time was spent in hunting and prospecting in Jessamine County, where two caves are still known as Boone's caves. Eventually, when ammunition and supplies had once more run low, Squire was compelled a second time to return to the settlements. Perturbed after a time by Squire's failure to rejoin him at the appointed time, Daniel started toward the settlements, in search of him; and by a stroke of good fortune encountered him along the trail. Overjoyed at this meeting (December, 1770) the indomitable Boones once more plunged into the wilderness, determined to conclude their explorations by examining the regions watered by the Green and Cumberland rivers and their tributaries. In after years, Gasper Mansker, the old German scout, was accustomed to describe with comic effect the consternation created among the Long Hunters, while hunting one day on Green River, by a singular noise which they could not explain. Stealthily slipping from tree to tree, Mansker finally beheld with mingled surprise and amusement a hunter, bareheaded, stretched flat upon his back on a deerskin spread on the ground, singing merrily at the top of his voice! It was Daniel Boone, joyously whiling away the solitary hours in singing one of his favorite songs of the border. In March, 1771, after spending some time in company with the Long Hunters, the Boones, their horses laden with furs, set their faces homeward. On their return journey, near Cumberland Gap, they had the misfortune to be surrounded by a party of Indians who robbed them of their guns and all their peltries. With this humiliating conclusion to his memorable tour of exploration, Daniel Boone, as he himself says, "once more reached home after experiencing hardships which would defy credulity in the recital."

Despite the hardships and the losses, Boone had achieved the ambition of years: he had seen Kentucky, which he "esteemed a second paradise." The reports of his extended explorations, which he made to Judge Henderson, were soon communicated to the other partners of the land company; and their letters of this period, to one another, bristle with glowing and minute descriptions of the country, as detailed by their agent. Boone was immediately engaged to act in the company's behalf to sound the Cherokees confidentially with respect to their willingness to lease or sell the beautiful hunting-grounds of the trans-Alleghany. The high hopes of Henderson and his associates at last gave promise of brilliant realization. Daniel Boone's glowing descriptions of Kentucky excited in their minds, says a gifted early chronicler, the "spirit of an enterprise which in point of magnitude and peril, as well as constancy and heroism displayed in its execution, has never been paralleled in the history of America."

CHAPTER XI. The Regulators

It is not a persons labour, nor yet his effects that will do, but if he has but one horse to plow with, one bed to lie on, or one cow to give a little milk for his children, they must all go to raise money which is not to be had. And lastly if his personal estate (sold at one tenth of its value) will not do, then his lands (which perhaps has cost him many years of toil and labour) must go the same way to satisfy, these cursed hungry caterpillars, that are eating and will eat out the bowels of our Commonwealth, if they be not pulled down from their nests in a very short time.—George Sims: A Serious Address to the Inhabitants of Granville County, containing an Account of our deplorable Situation we suffer .... and some necessary Hints with Respect to a Reformation. June 6, 1765.

It is highly probable that even at the time of his earlier explorations in behalf of Richard Henderson and Company, Daniel Boone anticipated speedy removal to the West. Indeed, in the very year of his first tour in their interest, Daniel and his wife Rebeckah sold all their property in North Carolina, consisting of their home and six hundred and forty acres of land, and after several removals established themselves upon the upper Yadkin. This removal and the later western explorations just outlined were due not merely to the spirit of adventure and discovery. Three other causes also were at work. In the first place there was the scarcity of game. For fifteen years the shipments of deerskins from Bethabara to Charleston steadily increased; and the number of skins bought by Gammern, the Moravian storekeeper, ran so high that in spite of the large purchases made at the store by the hunters he would sometimes run entirely out of money. Tireless in the chase, the far roaming Boone was among "the hunters, who brought in their skins from as far away as the Indian lands"; and the beautiful upland pastures and mountain forests, still teeming with deer and bear, doubtless lured him to the upper Yadkin, where for a time in the immediate neighborhood of his home abundance of game fell before his unerring rifle. Certainly the deer and other game, which were being killed in enormous numbers to satisfy the insatiable demand of the traders at Salisbury, the Forks, and Bethabara, became scarcer and scarcer; and the wild game that was left gradually fled to the westward. Terrible indeed was the havoc wrought among the elk; and it was reported that the last elk was killed in western North Carolina as early as 1781.

Another grave evil of the time with which Boone had to cope in the back country of North Carolina was the growth of undisguised outlawry, similar to that found on the western plains of a later era. This ruthless brigand age arose as the result of the unsettled state of the country and the exposed condition of the settlements due to the Indian alarms. When rude borderers, demoralized by the enforced idleness attendant upon fort life during the dark days of Indian invasion, sallied forth upon forays against the Indians, they found much valuable property—horses, cattle, and stock—left by their owners when hurriedly fleeing to the protection of the frontier stockades. The temptations thus afforded were too great to resist; and the wilder spirits of the backwoods, with hazy notions of private rights, seized the property which they found, slaughtered the cattle, sold the horses, and appropriated to their own use the temporarily abandoned household goods and plantation tools. The stealing of horses, which were needed for the cultivation of the soil and useful for quickly carrying unknown thieves beyond the reach of the owner and the law, became a common practice; and was carried on by bands of outlaws living remote from one another and acting in collusive concert.

Toward the end of July, 1755, when the Indian outrages upon the New River settlements in Virginia had frightened away all the families at the Town Fork in the Yadkin country, William Owen, a man of Welsh stock, who had settled in the spring of 1752 in the upper Yadkin near the Mulberry Fields, was suspected of having robbed the storekeeper on the Meho. Not long afterward a band of outlaws who plundered the exposed cabins in their owners' absence, erected a rude fort in the mountain region in the rear of the Yadkin settlements, where they stored their ill-gotten plunder and made themselves secure from attack. Other members of the band dwelt in the settlements, where they concealed their robber friends by day and aided them by night in their nefarious projects of theft and rapine.

The entire community was finally aroused by the bold depredations of the outlaws; and the most worthy settlers of the Yadkin country organized under the name of Regulators to break up the outlaw band. When it was discovered that Owen, who was well known at Bethabara, had allied himself with the highwaymen, one of the justices summoned one hundred men; and seventy, who answered the call, set forth on December 26, 1755, to seek out the outlaws and to destroy their fortress. Emboldened by their success, the latter upon one occasion had carried off a young girl of the settlements. Daniel Boone placed himself at the head of one of the parties, which included the young girl's father, to go to her rescue; and they fortunately succeeded in effecting the release of the frightened maiden. One of the robbers was apprehended and brought to Salisbury, where he was thrown into prison for his crimes. Meanwhile a large amount of plunder had been discovered at the house of one Cornelius Howard; and the evidences of his guilt so multiplied against him that he finally confessed his connection with the outlaw band and agreed to point out their fort in the mountains.

Daniel Boone and George Boone joined the party of seventy men, sent out by the colonial authorities under the guidance of Howard, to attack the stronghold of the bandits. Boone afterward related that the robbers' fort was situated in the most fitly chosen place for such a purpose that he could imagine—beneath an overhanging cliff of rock, with a large natural chimney, and a considerable area in front well stockaded. The frontiersmen surrounded the fort, captured five women and eleven children, and then burned the fort to the ground. Owen and his wife, Cumberland, and several others were ultimately made prisoners; but Harman and the remainder of the band escaped by flight. Owen and his fellow captives were then borne to Salisbury, incarcerated in the prison there, and finally (May, 1756) condemned to the gallows. Owen sent word to the Moravians, petitioning them to adopt his two boys and to apprentice one to a tailor, the other to a carpenter. But so infuriated was Owen's wife by Howard's treachery that she branded him as a second Judas; and this at once fixed upon him the sobriquet "Judas" Howard-a sobriquet he did not live long to bear, for about a year later he was ambushed and shot from his horse at the crossing of a stream. He thus paid the penalty of his betrayal of the outlaw band. For a number of years, the Regulators continued to wage war against the remaining outlaws, who from time to time committed murders as well as thefts. As late as January, 1768, the Regulators caught a horse thief in the Hollows of Surry County and brought him to Bethabara, whence Richter and Spach took him to the jail at Salisbury. After this year, the outlaws were heard of no more; and peace reigned in the settlements.

Colonel Edmund Fanning—of whom more anon—declared that the Regulation began in Anson County which bordered upon South Carolina. Certain it is that the upper country of that province was kept in an uproar by civil disturbances during this early period. Owing to the absence of courts in this section, so remote from Charleston, the inhabitants found it necessary, for the protection of property and the punishment of outlaws, to form an association called, like the North Carolina society, the Regulation. Against this association the horse thieves and other criminals made common cause, and received tacit support from certain more reputable persons who condemned "the irregularity of the Regulators." The Regulation which had been thus organized in upper South Carolina as early as 1764 led to tumultuous risings of the settlers; and finally in the effort to suppress these disorders, the governor, Lord Charles Montagu, appointed one Scovil, an utterly unworthy representative, to carry out his commands. After various disorders, which became ever more unendurable to the law-abiding, matters came to a crisis (1769) as the result of the high-handed proceedings of Scovil, who promiscuously seized and flung into prison all the Regulators he could lay hands on. In the month of March the back country rose in revolt against Scovil and a strong body of the settlers was on the point of attacking the force under his command when an eleventh-hour letter arrived from Montagu, dismissing Scovil from office. Thus was happily averted, by the narrowest of margins, a threatened precursor of the fight at Alamance in 1771 (see Chapter XII). As the result of the petition of the Calhouns and others, courts were established in 1760, though not opened until four years later. Many horse thieves were apprehended, tried, and punished. Justice once more held full sway.

Another important cause for Boone's removal from the neighborhood of Salisbury into the mountain fastnesses was the oppressive administration of the law by corrupt sheriffs, clerks, and tax-gatherers, and the dissatisfaction of the frontier squatters with the owners of the soil. At the close of the year 1764 reports reached the town of Wilmington, after the adjournment of the assembly in November, of serious disturbances in Orange County, due, it was alleged, to the exorbitant exactions of the clerks, registers, and some of the attorneys. As a result of this disturbing news, Governor Dobbs issued a proclamation forbidding any officer to take illegal fees. Troubles had been brewing in the adjacent county of Granville ever since the outbreak of the citizens against Francis Corbin, Lord Granville's agent (January 24, 1759), and the issuance of the petition of Reuben Searcy and others (March 23d) protesting against the alleged excessive fees taken and injustices practised by Robert (Robin) Jones, the famous lawyer. These disturbances were cumulative in their effect; and the people at last (1765) found in George Sims, of Granville, a fit spokesman of their cause and a doughty champion of popular rights. In his "Serious Address to the Inhabitants of Granville County, containing an Account of our deplorable Situation we suffer . . . and some necessary Hints with Respect to a Reformation," recently brought to light, he presents a crushing indictment of the clerk of the county court, Samuel Benton, the grandfather of Thomas Hart Benton. After describing in detail the system of semi-peonage created by the merciless exactions of lawyers and petty court officials, and the insatiable greed of "these cursed hungry caterpillars," Sims with rude eloquence calls upon the people to pull them down from their nests for the salvation of the Commonwealth.

Other abuses were also recorded. So exorbitant was the charge for a marriage-license, for instance, that an early chronicler records "The consequence was that some of the inhabitants on the head-waters of the Yadkin took a short cut. They took each other for better or for worse; and considered themselves as married without further ceremony." The extraordinary scarcity of currency throughout the colony, especially in the back country, was another great hardship and a perpetual source of vexation. All these conditions gradually became intolerable to the uncultured but free spirited men of the back country. Events were slowly converging toward a crisis in government and society. Independent in spirit, turbulent in action, the backwoodsmen revolted not only against excessive taxes, dishonest sheriffs, and extortionate fees, but also against the rapacious practices of the agents of Lord Granville. These agents industriously picked flaws in the titles to the lands in Granville's proprietary upon which the poorer settlers were seated; and compelled them to pay for the land if they had not already done so, or else to pay the fees twice over and take out a new patent as the only remedy of the alleged defect in their titles. In Mecklenburg County the spirit of backwoods revolt flamed out in protest against the proprietary agents. Acting under instructions to survey and close bargains for the lands or else to eject those who held them, Henry Eustace McCulloh, in February, 1765, went into the county to call a reckoning. The settlers, many of whom had located without deeds, indignantly retorted by offering to buy only at their own prices, and forbade the surveyors to lay out the holdings when this smaller price was declined. They not only terrorized into acquiescence those among them who were willing to pay the amount charged for the lands, but also openly declared that they would resist by force any sheriff in ejectment proceedings. On May 7th an outbreak occurred; and a mob, led by Thomas Polk, set upon John Frohock, Abraham Alexander, and others, as they were about to survey a parcel of land, and gave them a severe thrashing, even threatening the young McCulloh with death.

The choleric backwoodsmen, instinctively in agreement with Francis Bacon, considered revenge as a sort of wild justice. Especial objects of their animosity were the brothers Frohock, John and Thomas, the latter clerk of the court at Salisbury, and Edmund Fanning, a cultured gentleman-adventurer, associate justice of the superior court. So rapacious and extortionate were these vultures of the courts who preyed upon the vitals of the common people, that they were savagely lampooned by Rednap Howell, the backwoods poet-laureate of the Regulation. The temper of the back country is well caught in Howell's lines anent this early American "grafter", the favorite of the royal governor:

When Fanning first to Orange came,
He looked both pale and wan;
An old patched coat was on his back,
An old mare he rode on.

Both man and mare wan't worth five pounds,
As I've been often told;
But by his civil robberies,
He's laced his coat with gold.

The germs of the great westward migration in the coming decade were thus working among the people of the back country. If the tense nervous energy of the American people is the transmitted characteristic of the border settlers, who often slept with loaded rifle in hand in grim expectation of being awakened by the hideous yells, the deadly tomahawk, and the lurid firebrand of the savage, the very buoyancy of the national character is in equal measure "traceable to the free democracy founded on a freehold inheritance of land." The desire for free land was the fundamental factor in the development of the American democracy. No colony exhibited this tendency more signally than did North Carolina in the turbulent days of the Regulation. The North Carolina frontiersmen resented the obligation to pay quit-rents and firmly believed that the first occupant of the soil had an indefeasible right to the land which he had won with his rifle and rendered productive by the implements of toil. Preferring the dangers of the free wilderness to the paying of tribute to absentee landlords and officials of an intolerant colonial government, the frontiersman found title in his trusty rifle rather than in a piece of parchment, and was prone to pay his obligations to the owner of the soil in lead rather than in gold.

CHAPTER XII. Watauga—Haven of Liberty

The Regulators despaired of seeing better times and therefore quitted the Province. It is said 1,500 departed since the Battle of Alamance and to my knowledge a great many more are only waiting to dispose of their plantations in order to follow them.- - Reverend Morgan Edwards, 1772.

The five years (1766-1771) which saw the rise, development, and ultimate defeat of the popular movement known as the Regulation, constitute a period not only of extraordinary significance in North Carolina but also of fruitful consequences in the larger movements of westward expansion. With the resolute intention of having their rulers "give account of their stewardship," to employ their own words, the Sandy Creek Association of Baptists (organized in 1758), in a series of papers known as Regulators' Advertisements (1766-8) proceeded to mature, through popular gatherings, a rough form of initiative and referendum. At length, discouraged in its efforts, and particularly in the attempt to bring county officials to book for charging illegal fees, this association ceased actively to function. It was the precursor of a movement of much more drastic character and formidable proportions, chiefly directed against Colonel Edmund Fanning and his associates. This movement doubtless took its name, "the Regulation," from the bands of men already described who were organized first in North Carolina and later in South Carolina, to put down highwaymen and to correct many abuses in the back country, such as the tyrannies of Scovil and his henchmen. Failing to secure redress of their grievances through legal channels, the Regulators finally made such a powerful demonstration in support of their refusal to pay taxes that Governor William Tryon of North Carolina, in 1768, called out the provincial militia, and by marching with great show of force through the disaffected regions, succeeded temporarily in overawing the people and thus inducing them to pay their assessments.

The suits which had been brought by the Regulators against Edmund Fanning, register, and Francis Nash, clerk, of Orange County, resulted in both being "found guilty of taking too high fees." Fanning immediately resigned his commission as register; while Nash, who in conjunction with Fanning had fairly offered in 1766 to refund to any one aggrieved any fee charged by him which the Superior Court might hold excessive, gave bond for his appearance at the next court. Similar suits for extortion against the three Froliocks in Rowan County in 1769 met with failure, however; and this outcome aroused the bitter resentment of the Regulators, as recorded by Herman Husband in his "Impartial Relation." During this whole period the insurrectionary spirit of the people, who felt themselves deeply aggrieved but recognized their inability to secure redress, took the form of driving local justices from the bench and threatening court officials with violence.

At the session of the Superior Court at Hillsborough, September 22, 1770, an elaborate petition prepared by the Regulators, demanding unprejudiced juries and the public accounting for taxes by the sheriffs, was handed to the presiding justice by James Hunter, a leading Regulator. This justice was our acquaintance, Judge Richard Henderson, of Granville County, the sole high officer in the provincial government from the entire western section of the colony. In this petition occur these trenchant words: "As we are serious and in good earnest and the cause respects the whole body of the people it would be loss of time to enter into arguments on particular points for though there are a few men who have the gift and art of reasoning, yet every man has a feeling and knows when he has justice done him as well as the most learned." On the following Monday (September 24th), upon convening of court, some one hundred and fifty Regulators, led by James Hunter, Herman Husband, Rednap Howell, and others, armed with clubs, whips, and cudgels, surged into the court-room and through their spokesman, Jeremiah Fields, presented a statement of their grievances. "I found myself," says Judge Henderson, "under a necessity of attempting to soften and turn away the fury of these mad people, in the best manner in my power, and as such could well be, pacify their rage and at the same time preserve the little remaining dignity of the court."

During an interim, in which the Regulators retired for consultation, they fell without warning upon Fanning and gave him such rough treatment that he narrowly escaped with his life. The mob, now past control, horsewhipped a number of leading lawyers and citizens gathered there at court, and treated others, notably the courtly Mr. Hooper of Boston, "with every mark of contempt and insult." Judge Henderson was assured by Fields that no harm should come to him provided he would conduct the court in accordance with the behest of the Regulators: namely, that no lawyer, save the King's Attorney, should be admitted to the court, and that the Regulators' cases should be tried with new jurors chosen by the Regulators. With the entire little village terrorized by this campaign of "frightfulness," and the court wholly unprotected, Judge Henderson reluctantly acknowledged to himself that "the power of the judiciary was exhausted." Nevertheless, he says, "I made every effort in my power consistent with my office and the duty the public is entitled to claim to preserve peace and good order." Agreeing under duress to resume the session the following day, the judge ordered an adjournment. But being unwilling, on mature reflection, to permit a mockery of the court and a travesty of justice to be staged under threat and intimidation, he returned that night to his home in Granville and left the court adjourned in course. Enraged by the judge's escape, the Regulators took possession of the court room the following morning, called over the cases, and in futile protest against the conditions they were powerless to remedy, made profane entries which may still be seen on the record: "Damned rogues," "Fanning pays cost but loses nothing," "Negroes not worth a damn, Cost exceeds the whole," "Hogan pays and be damned," and, in a case of slander, "Nonsense, let them argue for Ferrell has gone hellward."

The uprising of these bold and resolute, simple and imperfectly educated people, which had begun as a constitutional struggle to secure justice and to prevent their own exploitation by dishonest lawyers of the county courts, now gave place to open anarchy and secret incendiarism. In the dead of night, November 12th and 14th, Judge Henderson's barn, stables, and dwelling house were fired by the Regulators and went up in flames. Glowing with a sense of wrong, these misguided people, led on by fanatical agitators, thus vented their indiscriminate rage, not only upon their oppressors, but also upon men wholly innocent of injuring them—men of the stamp of William Hooper, afterward signer of the Declaration of Independence, Alexander

Martin, afterward governor and United States Senator,,and Richard Henderson, popular representative of the back country and a firm champion of due process of law. It is perhaps not surprising in view of these events that Governor Tryon and the ruling class, lacking a sympathy broad enough to ensure justice to the oppressed people, seemed to be chiefly impressed with the fact that a widespread insurrection was in progress, threatening not only life and property, but also civil government itself. The governor called out the militia of the province and led an army of well nigh one thousand men and officers against the Regulators, who had assembled at Alamance to the number of two thousand. Tryon stood firm upon the demands that the people should submit to government and disperse at a designated hour. The Regulators, on their side, hoped to secure the reforms they desired by intimidating the governor with a great display of force. The battle was a tragic fiasco for the Regulators, who fought bravely, but without adequate arms or real leadership. With the conclusion of this desultory action, a fight lasting about two hours (May 16, 1771), the power of the Regulators was completely broken."

Among these insurgents there was a remarkable element, an element whose influence upon the course of American history has been but imperfectly understood which now looms into prominence as the vanguard of the army of westward expansion. There were some of the Regulators who, though law-abiding and conservative, were deeply imbued with ideas of liberty, personal independence, and the freedom of the soil. Through the influence of Benjamin Franklin, with whom one of the leaders of the group, Herman Husband, was in constant correspondence, the patriotic ideas then rapidly maturing into revolutionary sentiments furnished the inspiration to action. As early as 1766, the Sandy Creek leaders, referred to earlier in this chapter, issued a call to each neighborhood to send delegates to a gathering for the purpose of investigating the question "whether the free men of this country labor under any abuses of power or not." The close connection between the Sandy Creek men and the Sons of Liberty is amply demonstrated in this paper wherein the Sons of Liberty in connection with the "stamp law" are praised: for "redeeming us from Tyranny" and for having "withstood the lords in Parliament in behalf of true liberty." Upon the records of the Dutchman's Creek Church, of "regular" Baptists, at the Forks of the Yadkin, to which Daniel Boone's family belonged, may be found this memorable entry, recognizing the "American Cause" well-nigh a year before the declaration of independence at Philadelphia: "At the monthly meeting it was agreed upon concerning the American Cause, if any of the brethren see cause to join it they have the liberty to do it without being called to an account by the church. But whether they join or do not join they should be used with brotherly love.

The fundamental reasons underlying the approaching westward hegira are found in the remarkable petition of the Regulators of An son County (October 9, 1769), who request that "Benjamin Franklin or some other known *patriot*" be appointed agent of the province in London to seek redress at the source. They exposed the basic evil in the situation by pointing out that, in violation of the law restricting the amount of land that might be granted to each person to six hundred and forty acres, much of the most fertile territory in the province had been distributed in large tracts to wealthy landlords. In consequence "great numbers of poor people are necessitated to toil in the cultivation of the bad Lands whereon they hardly can subsist." It was these poor people, "thereby deprived of His Majesties liberality and Bounty," who soon turned their gaze to the westward and crossed the mountains in search of the rich, free lands of the trans-Alleghany region.

This feverish popular longing for freedom, stimulated by the economic pressure of thousands of pioneers who were annually entering North Carolina, set in motion a wave of migration across the mountains in 1769. Long before Alamance, many of the true Americans, distraught by apparently irremediable injustices, plunged fearlessly into the wilderness, seeking beyond the mountains a new birth of liberty, lands of their own selection free of cost or quit-rents, and a government of their own choosing and control."' The glad news of the rich valleys beyond the mountains early lured such adventurous pioneers as Andrew Greer and Julius Cæsar Dugger to the Watauga country. The glowing stories, told by Boone, and disseminated in the back country by Henderson, Williams, and the Harts, seemed to give promise to men of this stamp that the West afforded relief from oppressions suffered in North Carolina. During the winter of 1768-9 there was also a great rush of settlers from Virginia into the valley of the Holston. A party from Augusta County, led by men who had been delighted with the country viewed seven years before when they were serving under Colonel William Byrd against the Cherokees, found that this region, a wilderness on their outward passage in 1768, was dotted with cabins on every spot where the grazing was good, upon their return the following year. Writing to Hillsborough on October 18, 1770, concerning the "many hundred families" in the region from Green River to the branches of the Holston, who refused to comply with the royal proclamation of 1763, Acting-Governor Nelson of Virginia reports that "very little if any Quit Rents have been received for His Majesty's use from that Quarter for some time past"—the people claiming that "His Majesty hath been pleased to withdraw his protection from them since 1763."

In the spring of 1770, with the express intention of discovering suitable locations for homes for himself and a number of others, who wished to escape the accumulating evils of the times, James Robertson of Orange County, North Carolina, made an arduous journey to the pleasing valley of the Watauga. Robertson, who was born in Brunswick County, Virginia, June 28, 1742, of excellent Scotch-Irish ancestry, was a noteworthy figure of a certain type--quiet, reflective, conservative, wise, a firm believer in the basic principles of civil Liberty and the right of local self-government. Robertson spent some time with a man named Honeycut in the Watauga region, raised a crop of corn, and chose for himself and his friends suitable locations for settlement. Lost upon his return in seeking the mountain defiles traversed by him on the outward journey, Robertson probably escaped death from starvation only through the chance passing of two hunters who succored him and set him upon the right path. On arriving in Orange he found political and social conditions there much worse than before, many of the colonists declining to take the obligatory oath of allegiance to the British Crown after the Battle of Alamance, preferring to carve out for themselves new homes along the western waters. Some sixteen families of this stamp, indignant at the injustices and oppressions of British rule, and stirred by Robertson's description of the richness and beauty of the western country, accompanied him to Watauga shortly after the battle.

68

This vanguard of the army of westward advance, independent Americans in spirit with a negligible sprinkling of Loyalists, now swept in a great tide into the northeastern section of Tennessee. The men of Sandy Creek, actuated by independent principles but out of sympathy with the anarchic side of the Regulation, left the colony almost to a man. "After the defeat of the Regulators," says the historian of the Sandy Creek Association, "thousands of the oppressed, seeing no hope of redress for their grievances, moved into and settled east Tennessee. A large proportion of these were of the Baptist population. Sandy Creek Church which some time previous to 1771, numbered 606, was afterward reduced to fourteen members!" This movement exerted powerful influence in stimulating westward expansion. Indeed, it was from men of Regulating principles--Boone, Robertson, and the Searcys—who vehemently condemned the anarchy and incendiarism of 1770, that Judge Henderson received powerful cooperation in the opening up of Kentucky and Tennessee.

The several treaties concerning the western boundary of white settlement, concluded in close succession by North Carolina, Virginia, and the Crown with the Southern and Northern Indians, had an important bearing upon the settlement of Watauga. The Cherokee boundary line, as fixed by Governor Tryon (1767) and by John Stuart (1768), ran from Reedy River to Tryon Mountain, thence straight to Chiswell's Mine, and thence direct to the mouth of the Great Kanawha River. By the treaty at Fort Stanwix (November 5, 1768), in the negotiation of which Virginia was represented by Dr. Thomas Walker and Major Andrew Lewis, the Six Nations sold to the Crown their shadowy claim to a vast tract of western country, including in particular all the land between the Ohio and the Tennessee Rivers. The news of the cession resulted in a strong southwestward thrust of population, from the neighborhood of Abingdon, in the direction of the Holston Valley. Recognizing that hundreds of these settlers were beyond the line negotiated by Stuart, but on lands not yet surveyed, Governor Botetourt instructed the Virginia commissioners to press for further negotiations, through Stuart, with the Cherokees. Accordingly, on October 18, 1770, a new treaty was made at Lochaber, South Carolina, by which a new line back of Virginia was established, beginning at the intersection of the North Carolina-Cherokee line (a point some seventy odd miles east of Long Island), running thence in a west course to a point six miles east of Long Island, and thence in a direct course to the confluence of the Great Kanawha and Ohio Rivers. At the time of the treaty, it was agreed that the Holston River, from its intersection with the North Carolina-Virginia line, and down the course of the same, should be a temporary southern boundary of Virginia until the line should be ascertained by actual survey. A strong influx of population into the immense new triangle thus released for settlement brought powerful pressure to bear upon northern Tennessee, the point of least resistance along the western barrier. Singularly enough, this advance was not opposed by the Cherokees, whose towns were strung across the extreme southeast corner of Tennessee.

When Colonel John Donelson ran the line in the latter part of 1771, The Little Carpenter, who with other Indian chiefs accompanied the surveying party, urged that the line agreed upon at Lochaber should break off at the head of the Louisa River, and should run thence to the mouth thereof, and thence up the Ohio to the mouth of the Great Kanawha. For this increase in the territory of Virginia they of course expected additional payment. As a representative of Virginia, Donelson agreed to the proposed alteration in the boundary line; and accordingly promised to send the Cherokees, in the following spring, a sum alleged by them to have been fixed at five hundred pounds, in compensation for the additional area. This informal agreement, it is believed, was never ratified by Virginia; nor was the promised compensation ever paid the Cherokees.

Under the belief that the land belonged to Virginia, Jacob Brown with one or two families from North Carolina settled in 1771 upon a tract of land on the northern bank of the Nonachunheh (corruption, Nolichucky) River. During the same year, an experimental line run westward from Steep Rock and Beaver Creek by Anthony Bledsoe showed that upon the extension of the boundary line, these settlers would fall within the bounds of North Carolina. Although thus informally warned of the situation, the settlers made no move to vacate the lands. But in the following year, after the running of Donelson's line, Alexander Cameron, Stuart's deputy, required "all persons who had made settlements beyond the said line to relinquish them." Thus officially warned, Brown and his companions removed to Watauga. Cameron's order did not apply, however, to the settlement, to the settlement north of the Holston River, south and east of Long Island; and the settlement in Carter's Valley, although lying without the Virginia boundary, strangely enough remained unmolested. The order was directed at the Watauga settlers, who were seated south of the Holston River in the Watauga Valley.

The plight in which the Watauga settlers now found themselves was truly desperate; and the way in which they surmounted this apparently insuperable difficulty is one of the most striking and characteristic events in the pre-Revolutionary history of the Old Southwest. It exhibits the indomitable will and fertile resource of the American character at the margin of desperation. The momentous influence of the Watauga settlers, inadequately reckoned hitherto by historians, was soon to make itself powerfully felt in the first epochal movement of westward expansion.

70

CHAPTER XIII. Opening the Gateway—Dunmore's War

Virginia, we conceive, can claim this Country [Kentucky] with the greatest justice and propriety, its within the Limits of their Charter. They Fought and bled for it. And had it not been for the memorable Battle, at the Great Kanaway those vast regions had yet continued inaccessable.—The Harrodsburg Petition. June 7-15, 1776.

It was fortunate for the Watauga settlers that the Indians and the whites were on the most peaceful terms with each other at the time the Watauga Valley was shown, by the running of the boundary line, to lie within the Indian reservation. With true American self reliance, the settlers met together for deliberation and counsel, and deputed James Robertson and John Been, as stated by Tennessee's first historian, "to treat with their landlords, and agree upon articles of accommodation and friendship. The attempt succeeded. For though the Indians refused to give up the land gratuitously, they consented, for a stipulated amount of merchandise, muskets, and other articles of convenience, to lease all the country on the waters of the Watauga." In addition to the land thus leased for ten years, several other tracts were purchased from the Indians by Jacob Brown, who reoccupied his former location on the Nolichucky.

In taking this daring step, the Watauga settlers moved into the spotlight of national history. For the inevitable consequence of leasing the territory was the organization of a form of government for the infant settlement. Through his familiarity with the North Carolina type of "association," in which the settlers had organized for the purpose of "regulating" abuses, and his acquaintance with the contents of the "Impartial Relation," in which Husband fully expounded the principles and practices of this association, Robertson was peculiarly fitted for leadership in organizing this new government. The convention at which Articles of Association, unfortunately lost, were drawn up, is noteworthy as the first governmental assemblage of free-born American citizens ever held west of the Alleghanies. The government then established was the first free and independent government, democratic in spirit, representative in form, ever organized upon the American continent. In describing this mimic republic, the royal Governor of Virginia says: "They appointed magistrates, and framed laws for their present occasion, and to all intents and purposes, erected themselves into, though an inconsiderable, yet a separate State." The most daring spirit in this little state was the young John Sevier, of French Huguenot family (originally spelled Xavier), born in Augusta County, Virginia, on September 23, 1745. It was from Millerstown in Shenandoah County where he was living the uneventful life of a small farmer, that he emigrated (December, 1773) to the Watauga region. With his arrival there begins one of the most fascinating and romantic careers recorded in the varied arid stirring annals of the Old Southwest. In this daring and impetuous young fellow, fair-haired, blue-eyed, magnetic, debonair—of powerful build, splendid proportions, and athletic skill—we hold the gallant exemplar of the truly heroic life of the border. The story of his life, thrilling in the extreme, is rich in all the multi-colored elements which impart romance to the arduous struggle of American civilization in the opening years of the republic.

The creative impulses in the Watauga commonwealth are hinted at by Dunmore, who serves, in the letter above quoted, that Watauga "sets a dangerous example to the people America, of forming governments distinct from and independent of his Majesty's authority."

It is true that the experiment was somewhat limited. The organization of the Watauga association, which constituted a temporary expedient to meet a crisis in the affairs of a frontier community cut off by forest wilderness and mountain barriers from the reach of the arm of royal or provincial government, is not to be compared with the revolutionary assemblage at Boonesborough, May 23, 1775, or with the extraordinary demands for inde pendence in Mecklenburg County, North Carolina, during the same month. Nevertheless the Watauga settlers defied both North Carolina and the Crown, by adopting the laws of Virginia and by ignoring Governor Josiah Martin's proclamation (March 26, 1774) "requiring the said settlers immediately to retire from the Indian Territories." Moreover, Watauga really was the parent of a series of mimic republics in the Old Southwest, gradually tending toward higher forms of organization, with a larger measure of individual liberty. Watauga, Transylvania, Cumberland, Franklin represent the evolving political genius of a free people under the creative leadership of three constructive minds—James Robertson, John Sevier, and Richard Henderson. Indeed, Watauga furnished to Judge Henderson precisely the "dangerous example" of which Dunmore prophetically speaks.

Immediately upon his return in 1771 from the extended exploration of Kentucky, Daniel Boone as already noted was engaged as secret agent, to treat with the Cherokees for the lease or purchase of the trans-Alleghany region, on behalf of Judge Henderson and his associates. Embroiled in the exciting issues of the Regulation and absorbed by his confining duties as colonial judge, Henderson was unable to put his bold design into execution until after the expiration of the court itself which ceased to exist in 1773. Disregarding the royal proclamation of 1763 and Locke's Fundamental Constitutions for the Carolinas, which forbade private parties to purchase lands from the Indians, Judge Henderson applied to the highest judicial authorities in England to know if there was any law in existence forbidding purchase of lands from the Indian tribes. Lord Mansfield gave Judge Henderson the "sanction of his great authority in favor of the purchase." Lord Chancellor Camden and Mr. Yorke had officially advised the King in 1757, in regard to the petition of the East Indian Company, "that in respect to such territories as have been, or shall be acquired by treaty or grant from the Great Mogul, or any of the Indian princes or governments, your Majesty's letters patent are *not necessary*; the property of the soil vesting in the company by the Indian grant subject only to your Majesties right of sovereignty over the settlements, as English settlements, and over the inhabitants, as English subjects, who carry with them your Majesties laws wherever they form colonies, and receive your Majesties protection by virtue of your royal charters." This opinion, with virtually no change, was rendered in regard to the Indian tribes of North America by the same two authorities, certainly as early as 1769; and a true copy, made in London, April 1, 1772, was transmitted to Judge Henderson. Armed with the legal opinions received from England, Judge Henderson was fully persuaded that there was no legal bar whatsoever to his seeking to acquire by purchase from the Cherokees the vast domain of the trans-Alleghany. A golden dream of empire, with its promise of an independent republic in the form of a proprietary colony, casts him under the spell of its alluring glamour.

In the meantime, the restless Boone, impatient over the delay in the consummation of Judge Henderson's plans, resolved to establish himself in Kentucky upon his own responsibility. Heedless of the question of title and the certain hazards incident to invading the territory of hostile savages, Boone designated a rendezvous in Powell's Valley where he and his party of five families were to be met by a band under the leadership of his connections, the Bryans, and another company led by Captain William Russell, a daring pioneer of the Clinch Valley. A small detachment of Boone's party was fiercely attacked by Shawanoes in Powell's Valley on October 10, 1773, and almost all were killed, including sons of Boone and Russell, and young John and Richard Mendenhall of Guilford County, North Carolina. As the result of this bloody repulse, Boone's attempt to settle in Kentucky at this time was definitely abandoned. His failure to effect a settlement in Kentucky was due to that characteristic disregard of the territorial rights of the Indians which was all too common among the borderers of that period.

This failure was portentous of the coming storm. The reign of the Long Hunters was over. Dawning upon the horizon was the day of stern adventurers, fixed in the desperate and lawless resolve to invade the trans-Alleghany country and to battle savagely with the red man for its possession. More successful than Boone was the McAfee party, five in number, from Botetourt County, Virginia, who between May 10th and September 1, 1773, safely accomplished a journey through Kentucky and carefully marked well-chosen sites for future location." An ominous incident of the time was the veiled warning which Cornstalk, the great Shawanoe chieftain, gave to Captain Thomas Bullitt, head of a party of royal surveyors, sent out by Lord Dunmore, Governor of Virginia. Cornstalk at Chillicothe, June 7, 1773, warned Bullitt concerning the encroachments of the whites, "designed to deprive us," he said, "of the hunting of the country, as usual . . . the hunting we stand in need of to buy our clothing." During the preceding summer, George Rogers Clark, an aggressive young Virginian, with a small party, had descended the Ohio as low as Fish Creek, where he built a cabin; and in this region for many months various parties of surveyors were busily engaged in locating and surveying lands covered by military grants. Most significant of the ruthless determination of the pioneers to occupy by force the Kentucky area was the action of the large party from Monongahela, some forty in number, led by Captain James Harrod, who penetrated to the present Miller County, where in June, 1774, they made improvements and actually laid out a town.

A significant, secretly conducted movement, of which historians have taken but little account, was now in progress under the manipulation of Virginia's royal governor. As early as 1770 Dr. John Connolly proposed the establishment of an extensive colony south of the Ohio; and the design of securing such territory from the Indians found lodgment in the mind of Lord Dunmore. But this design was for the moment thwarted when on October 28, 1773, an order was issued from the Privy Council chamber in Whitehall granting an immense territory, including all of the present West Virginia and the land alienated to Virginia by Donelson's agreement with the Cherokees (1772), to a company including Thomas Walpole, Samuel Wharton, Benjamin Franklin, and others. This new colony, to be named "Vandalia," seemed assured. A clash between Dunmore and the royal authorities was imminent; for Virginia under her sea-to-sea charter claimed the vast middle region of the continent, extending without known limit to west and northwest. Moreover, Dunmore was interested in great land speculations on his own account; and while overtly vindicating Virginia's claim to the trans-Alleghany by despatching parties of surveyors to the western wilderness to locate and survey lands covered by military grants, he with the collusion of certain members of the "Honourable Board," his council, as charged by Washington, was more than "lukewarm," secretly restricting as rigorously as he dared the extent and number of the soldiers' allotments. According to the famous Virginia Remonstrance, he was in league with "men of great influence in some of the neighboring states" to secure, under cover of purchases from the Indians, large tracts of country between the Ohio and the Mississippi." In shaping his plans Dunmore had the shrewd legal counsel of Patrick Henry, who was equally intent upon making for himself a private purchase from the Cherokees. It was Henry's legal opinion that the Indiana purchase from the Six Nations by the Pennsylvania traders at Fort Stanwix (November 5, 1768) was valid; and that purchase by private individuals from the Indians gave full and ample title. In consequence of these facts, William Murray, in behalf of himself and his associates of the Illinois Land Company, and on the strength of the Camden Yorke decision, purchased two large tracts, on the Illinois and Ohio respectively, from the Illinois Indians (July 5, 1773); and in order to win the support of Dunmore, who was ambitious to make a fortune in land speculation, organized a second company, the Wabash (Ouabache) Land Company, with the governor as the chief share-holder. In response to Murray's petition on behalf of the Illinois Land Company, Dunmore (May, 1774) recommended it to Lord Dartmouth, Secretary of State for the Colonies, and urged that it be granted; and in a later letter he disingenuously disclaimed any personal interest in the Illinois speculation.

The party of surveyors sent out under the direction of Colonel William Preston, on the request of Washington and other leading eastern men, in 1774 located lands covered by military grants on the Ohio and in the Kentucky area for prominent Virginians, including Washington, Patrick Henry, William Byrd, William Preston, Arthur Campbell, William Fleming, and Andrew Lewis, among others, and also a large tract for Dr. Connolly. Certain of these grants fell within the Vandalia area; and in his reply (September 10, 1774) to Dunmore's letter, Lord Dartmouth sternly censured Dunmore for allowing these grants, and accused the white settlers of having brought on, by such unwarrantable aggressions, the war then raging with the Indians. This charge lay at the door of Dunmore himself; and there is strong evidence that Dunmore personally fomented the war, ostensibly in support of Virginia's charter rights, but actually in order to further his own speculative designs." Dunmore's agent, Dr. Connolly, heading a party posing as Virginia militia, fired without provocation upon a delegation of Shawanoe chiefs assembled at Fort Pitt (January, 1774). Taking advantage of the alarming situation created by the conflict of the claims of Virginia and Pennsylvania, Connolly, inspired by Dunmore without doubt, then issued an incendiary circular (April 21, 1774), declaring a state of war to exist. Just two weeks before the Battle of the Great Kanawha, Patrick Henry categorically stated, in conversation with Thomas Wharton:

"that he was at Williamsburg with Ld. D. when Dr. Conolly first came there, that Conolly is a chatty, sensible man, and informed Ld. Dunmore of the extreme richness of the lands which lay on both sides of the Ohio; that the prohibitory orders which had been sent him relative to the land on the hither side (or Vandalia) had caused him to turn his thoughts to the opposite shore, and that as his Lordship was determined to settle his family in America he was really pursueing this war, in order to obtain by purchase or treaty from the natives a tract of territory on that side; he then told me that he was convinced from every authority that the law knew, that a purchase from the natives was as full and ample a title as could be obtained, that they had Lord Camden and Mr. York's opinion on that head, which opinion with some others that Ld. Dunmore had consulted, and with the knowledge Conolly had given him of the quality of the country and his determined resolution to settle his family on this continent, were the real motives or springs of the present expedition."

At this very time, Patrick Henry, in conjunction with William Byrd 3d and others, was negotiating for a private purchase of lands from the Cherokees; and when Wharton, after answering Henry's inquiry as to where he might buy Indian goods, remarked: "It's not possible you mean to enter the Indian trade at this period," Henry laughingly replied: "The wish-world is my hobby horse." "From whence I conclude," adds Wharton, "he has some prospect of making a purchase of the natives, but where I know not."

The war, thus promulgated, we believe, at Dunmore's secret instigation and heralded by a series of ghastly atrocities, came on apace. After the inhuman murder of the family of Logan, the Indian chieftain, by one Greathouse and his drunken companions (April 30th), Logan, who contrary to romantic views was a blackhearted and vengeful savage, harried the Tennessee and Virginia borders, burning and slaughtering. Unable to arouse the Cherokees, owing to the opposition of Atta-kulla-kulla, Logan as late as July 21st said in a letter to the whites: "The Indians are not angry, only myself," and not until then did Dunmore begin to give full execution to his warlike plans. The best woodsmen of the border, Daniel Boone and the German scout Michael Stoner, having been despatched on July 27th by Colonel William Preston to warn the surveyors of the trans-Alleghany, made a remarkable journey on foot of eight hundred miles in sixty-one days. Harrod's company at Harrodsburg, a company of surveyors at Fontainebleau, Floyd's party on the Kentucky, and the surveyors at Mann's Lick, this warned, hurried in to the settlements and were saved. Meanwhile, Dunmore, in command of the Virginia forces, invaded territory guaranteed to the Indians by the royal proclamation of 1763 and recently (1774) added to the province of Quebec, a fact of which he was not aware, conducted a vigorous campaign, and fortified Camp Charlotte, near Old Chillicothe. Andrew Lewis, however, in charge of the other division of Dunmore's army, was the one destined to bear the real brunt and burden of the campaign. His division, recruited from the very flower of the pioneers of the Old Southwest, was the most representative body of borderers of this region that up to this time had assembled to measure strength with the red men. It was an army of the true stalwarts of the frontier, with fringed leggings and hunting-capes, rifles and powder-horns, hunting-knives and tomahawks.

The Battle of the Great Kanawha, at Point Pleasant, was fought on October 10, 1774, between Lewis's force, eleven hundred strong, and the Indians, under Cornstalk, somewhat inferior in numbers. It was a desultory action, over a greatly extended front and in very brushy country between Crooked Creek and the Ohio. Throughout the long day, the Indians fought with rare craft and stubborn bravery—loudly cursing the white men, cleverly picking off their leaders, and derisively inquiring, in regard to the absence of the fifes: "Where are your whistles now?" Slowly retreating, they sought to draw the whites into an ambuscade and at a favorable moment to "drive the Long Knives like bullocks into the river." No marked success was achieved on either side until near sunset, when a flank movement directed by young Isaac Shelby alarmed the Indians, who mistook this party for the expected reinforcement under Christian, and retired across the Ohio. In the morning the whites were amazed to discover that the Indians, who the preceding day so splendidly heeded the echoing call of Cornstalk, "Be strong! Be strong!", had quit the battlefield and left the victory with the whites.

The peace negotiated by Dunmore was durable. The governor had accomplished his purpose, defied the authority of the crown, and

vindicated the claim of Virginia, to the enthusiastic satisfaction of the backwoodsmen. While tendering their thanks to him and avowing their allegiance to George III, at the close of the campaign, the borderers proclaimed their resolution to exert all their powers "for the defense of American liberty, and for the support of her just rights and privileges, not in any precipitous, riotous or tumultuous manner, but when regularly called forth by the unanimous voice of our countrymen." Dunmore's War is epochal, in that it procured for the nonce a state of peace with the Indians, which made possible the advance of Judge Henderson over the Transylvania Trail in 1775, and, through his establishment of the Transylvania Fort at Boonesborough, the ultimate acquisition by the American Confederation of the imperial domain of the trans-Alleghany.

CHAPTER XIV. Richard Henderson and the Transylvania Company

> I happened to fall in company, and have a great deal of conversation with one of the most singular and extraordinary persons and excentric geniuses in America, and perhaps in the world. His name is Richard Henderson.—J. F. D. Smyth: A Tour in the United States of America.

Early in 1774, chastened by his own disastrous failure the preceding autumn, Boone advised Judge Henderson that the time was auspicious for opening negotiations with the Cherokees for purchasing the trans-Alleghany region." In organizing a company for this purpose, Henderson chose men of action and resource, leaders in the colony, ready for any hazard of life and fortune in this gigantic scheme of colonization and promotion. The new men included, in addition to the partners in the organization known as Richard Henderson and Company, were Colonel John Luttrell, destined to win laurels in the Revolution, and William Johnston, a native of Scotland, the leading merchant of Hillsborough.

Meeting in Hillsborough on August 27, 1774, these men organized the new company under the name of the Louisa Company. In the articles then drawn up they agreed to "rent or purchase" a tract of land from the Indian owners of the soil for the express purpose of "settling the country." Each partner obligated himself to "furnish his Quota of Expenses necessary towards procuring the grant." In full anticipation of the grave dangers to be encountered, they solemnly bound themselves, as "equal sharers in the property," to "support each other with our lives and fortunes." Negotiations with the Indians were begun at once. Accompanied by Colonel Nathaniel Hart and guided by the experienced Indian-trader, Thomas Price, Judge Henderson visited the Cherokee chieftains at the Otari towns. After elaborate consultations, the latter deputed the old chieftain, Atta-kulla-kulla, a young buck, and a squaw, "to attend the said Henderson and Hart to North Carolina, and there examine the Goods and Merchandize which had been by them offered as the Consideration of the purchase." The goods purchased at Cross Creek (now Fayetteville, North Carolina), in which the Louisa Company "had embarked a large amount," met the entire approval of the Indians—the squaw in particular shrewdly examining the goods in the interest of the women of the tribe.

On January 6, 1775, the company was again enlarged, and given the name of the Transylvania Company-the three new partners being David Hart, brother to Thomas and Nathaniel, Leonard Henley Bullock, a prominent citizen of Granville, and James Hogg, of Hillsborough, a native Scotchman and one of the most influential men in the colony. In the elaborate agreement drawn up reference is explicitly made to the contingency of "settling and voting as a proprietor and giving Rules and Regulations for the Inhabitants *etc.*" Hillsborough was the actual starting-point for the westward movement, the first emigrants, traveling thence to the Sycamore Shoals of the Watauga. In speaking of the departure of the settlers, the first movement of extended and permanent westward migration, an eye-witness quaintly says: "At this place [Hillsborough] I saw the first party of emigrant families that moved to Kentucky under the auspices of Judge Henderson. They marched out of the town with considerable solemnity, and to many their destination seemed as remote as if it had been to the South Sea Islands." Meanwhile, the "Proposals for the encouragement of settling the lands *etc.*," issued on Christmas Day, 1774, were quickly spread broadcast through the colony and along the border." It was the greatest sensation North Carolina had known since Alamance; and Archibald Neilson, deputy-auditor and naval officer of the colony, inquired with quizzical anxiety: "Pray, is Dick Henderson out of his head?" The most liberal terms, proffered by one quite in possession of his head, were embodied in these proposals. Land at twenty shillings per hundred acres was offered to each emigrant settling within the territory and raising a crop of corn before September 1, 1775, the emigrant being permitted to take up as much as five hundred acres for him self and two hundred and fifty acres for each tithable person under him. In these "Proposals" there was no indication that the low terms at which the lands were offered would be maintained after September 1, 1775. In a letter to Governor Dunmore (January, 1775), Colonel William Preston, county surveyor of Fincastle County, Virginia, says "The low price he [Henderson] proposes to sell at, together with some further encouragement he offers, will I am apprehensive induce a great many families to remove from this County (Fincastle) & Carolina and settle there." Joseph Martin, states his son, "was appointed entry-Taker and agent for the Powell Valley portion" of the Transylvania Purchase on January 20, 1775; and "he (Joseph Martin) and others went on in the early part of the year 1775 and made their stand at the very spot where he had made corn several years before. In speaking of the startling design, unmasked by Henderson, of establishing an independent government, Colonel Preston writes to George Washington of the contemplated "large Purchase by one Col. Henderson of North Carolina from the Cherokees . . . . I hear that Henderson talks with great Freedom & Indecency of the Governor of Virginia, sets the Government at Defiance & says if he once had five hundred good Fellows settled in that Country he would not Value Virginia."

Early in 1775 runners were sent off to the Cherokee towns to summon the Indians to the treaty ground at the Sycamore Shoals of the Watauga; and Boone, after his return from a hunt in Kentucky in January, was summoned by Judge Henderson to aid in the negotiations preliminary to the actual treaty. The dominating figure in the remarkable assemblage at the treaty ground, consisting of twelve hundred Indians and several hundred whites, was Richard Henderson, "comely in person, of a benign and social disposition," with countenance betokening the man of strenuous action" noble forehead, prominent nose, projecting chin, firm-set jaw, with kindness and openness of expression." Gathered about him, picturesque in garb and striking in appearance, were many of the buckskin-clad leaders of the border—James Robertson, John Sevier, Isaac Shelby, William Bailey Smith, and their compeers—as well as his Carolina friends John Williams, Thomas and Nathaniel Hart, Nathaniel Henderson, Jesse Benton,and Valentine Searcy.

Little was accomplished on the first day of the treaty (March 14th); but on the next day, the Cherokees offered to sell the section bargained for by Donelson acting as agent for Virginia in 1771. Although the Indians pointed out that Virginia had never paid the promised compensation of five hundred pounds and had therefore forfeited her rights, Henderson flatly refused to entertain the idea of purchasing territory to which Virginia had the prior claim. Angered by Henderson's refusal, The Dragging Canoe, leaping into the circle of the seated savages, made an impassioned speech touched with the romantic imagination peculiar to the American Indian. With pathetic eloquence he dwelt upon the insatiable land-greed of the white men, and predicted the extinction of his race if they committed the insensate folly of selling their beloved hunting-grounds. Roused to a high pitch of oratorical fervor, the savage with uplifted arm fiercely exhorted his people to resist further encroachments at all hazards—and left the treaty ground. This incident brought the conference to a startling and abrupt conclusion. On the following day, however, the savages proved more tractable,agreeing to sell the land as far as the Cumberland River. In order to secure the additional territory watered by the tributaries of the Cumberland, Henderson agreed to pay an additional sum of two thousand pounds. Upon this day there originated the ominous phrase descriptive of Kentucky when The Dragging Canoe, dramatically pointing toward the west, declared that a *dark* Cloud hung over that land, which was known as the *bloody ground*.

On the last day, March 17th, the negotiations were opened with the signing of the "Great Grant." The area purchased, some twenty millions of acres, included almost all the present state of Kentucky, and an immense tract in Tennessee, comprising all the territory watered by the Cumberland River and all its tributaries. For "two thousand weight of leather in goods" Henderson purchased "the lands lying down Holston and between the Watauga lease, Colonel Donelson's line and Powell's Mountain" as a pathway to Kentucky -the deed for which was known as the "Path Deed." By special arrangement, Carter's Valley in this tract went to Carter and Lucas; two days later, for two thousand pounds, Charles Robertson on behalf of the Watauga Association purchased a large tract in the valleys of the Holston, Watauga, and New Rivers; and eight days later Jacob Brown purchased two large areas, including the Nolichucky Valley. This historic treaty, which heralds the opening of the West, was conducted with absolute justice and fairness by Judge Henderson and his associates. No liquor was permitted at the treaty ground; and Thomas Price, the ablest of the Cherokee traders, deposed that "he at that time understood the Cherokee language, so as to comprehend everything which was said and to know that what was observed on either side was fairly and truly translated; that the Cherokees perfectly understood, what Lands were the subject of the Treaty . . . ." The amount paid by the Transylvania Company for the imperial domain was ten thousand pounds sterling, in money and in goods.

Although Daniel Boone doubtless assisted in the proceedings prior to the negotiation of the treaty, his name nowhere appears in the voluminous records of the conference. Indeed, he was not then present; for a fortnight before the conclusion of the treaty he was commissioned by Judge Henderson to form a party of competent woodmen to blaze a passage through the wilderness. On March 10th this party of thirty ax-men, under the leadership of Boone, started from the rendezvous, the Long Island of Holston, to engage in the arduous labor of cutting out the Transylvania Trail.

Henderson, the empire-builder, now faced with courage and resolution the hazardous task of occupying the purchased territory and establishing an independent government. No mere financial promoter of a vast speculative enterprise, he was one of the heroic figures of the Old Southwest; and it was his dauntless courage, his unwavering resolve to go forward in the face of all dangers, which carried through the armed "trek" to a successful conclusion. At Martin's Station, where Henderson and his party tarried to build a house in which to store their wagons, as the road could be cleared no further, they were joined by another party, of five adventurers from Prince William County, Virginia." In Henderson's party were some forty men and boys, with forty packhorses and a small amount of powder, lead, salt, and garden-seeds. The warning freely given by Joseph Martin of the perils of the path was soon confirmed, as appears from the following entry in Henderson's diary:

"Friday the 7th. [April] About Brake of Day began to snow. About 11 O'Clock received a letter from Mr. Luttrells camp that were five persons killd on the road to the Cantuckie by Indians. Capt. [Nathaniel] Hart, uppon the receipt of this News Retreated back with his Company, & determined to Settle in the Valley to make Corn for the Cantucky people. The same Day Received a Letter from Dan. Boone, that his Company was fired uppon by Indians, Kill'd Two of his men—tho he kept the ground & saved the Baggage &c."

The following historic letter, which reveals alike the dogged resolution of Boone and his reliance upon Henderson and his company in this black hour of disaster, addressed "Colonel Richard Henderson—these with care," is eloquent in its simplicity

"Dear Colonel: After my compliments to you, I shall acquaint you of our misfortunes. On March the 25 a party of Indians fired on my Company about half an hour before day, and killed Mr. Twitty and his negro, and wounded Mr. Walker very deeply, but I hope he will recover.

"On March the 28 as we were hunting for provisions, we found Samuel Tate's son, who gave us an account that the Indians fired on their camp on the 27th day. My brother and I went down and found two men killed and sculped, Thomas McDowell and Jeremiah McFeters. I have sent a man down to all the lower companies in order to gather them all at the mouth of Otter Creek.

"My advice to you, Sir, is to come or send as soon as possible. Your company is desired greatly, for the people are very uneasy, but are willing to stay and venture their lives with you. and now is the time to flusterate their [the Indians'] intentions, and keep the country, whilst we are in it. If we give way to them now, it will ever be the case. This day we start from the battle ground, for the mouth of Otter Creek, where we shall immediately erect a Fort, which will be done before you can come or send, then we can send ten men to meet you, if you send for them.

"I am, Sir, your most obedient
    Omble Sarvent
Daniel Boone.

"N.B. We stood on the ground and guarded our baggage till day, and lost nothing.
We have about fifteen miles to Cantuck [Kentucky River] at Otter Creek."

This dread intelligence caused the hearts of strong men to quail and induced some to
turn back, but Henderson, the jurist-pioneer, was made of sterner stuff. At once
(April 8th) he despatched an urgent letter in hot haste to the proprietors of
Transylvania, enclosing Boone's letter, informing them of Boone's plight and urging
them to send him immediately a large quantity of powder and lead, as he had been
compelled to abandon his supply of saltpeter at Martin's Station. "We are all in high
spirits," he assures the proprietors, "and on thorns to fly to Boone's assistance, and
join him in defense of so fine and valuable a country."

Laconically eloquent is this simple entry in his diary: "Saturday the 8th. Started abt.
10 oClock Crossed Cumberland Gap about 4 miles met about 40 persons Returning
from the Cantucky, on Acct. of the Late Murders by the Indians could prevail on one
only to return. Memo Several Virginians who were with us return'd."

There is no more crucial moment in early Western history than this, in which we see
the towering form of Henderson, clad in the picturesque garb of the pioneer, with
outstretched arm resolutely pointing forward to the "dark and bloody ground," and in
impassioned but futile eloquence pleading with the pale and panic-stricken fugitives
to turn about, to join his company, and to face once more the mortal dangers of
pioneer conquest. Significant indeed are the lines:

Some to endure, and many to fail,
Some to conquer, and many to quail,
Toiling over the Wilderness Trail.

The spirit of the pioneer knight-errant inspires Henderson's words: "In this situation,
some few, of genuine courage and undaunted resolution, served to inspire the rest; by
the help of whose example, assisted by a little pride and some ostentation, we made a
shift to march on with all the appearance of gallantry, and, cavalier like, treated
every insinuation of danger with the utmost contempt."

Fearing that Boone, who did not even know that Henderson's cavalcade was on the
road, would be unable to hold out, Henderson realized the imperative necessity for
sending him a message of encouragement. The bold young Virginian, William
Cocke, volunteered to brave alone the dangers of the murder-haunted trail to
undertake a ride more truly memorable and hazardous than that of Revere. "This
offer, extraordinary as it was, we could by no means refuse," remarks Henderson,
who shed tears of gratitude as he proffered his sincere thanks and wrung the brave
messenger's hand. Equipped with "a good Queen Anne's musket, plenty of
ammunition, a tomahawk, a large cuttoe knife [French, couteau], a Dutch blanket,

and no small quantity of jerked beef," Cocke on April 10th rode off "to the Cantuckey to Inform Capt Boone that we were on the road." The fearful apprehensions felt for Cocke's safety were later relieved, when along the road were discovered his letters in forming Henderson of his arrival and of his having been joined on the way by Page Portwood of Rowan. On his arrival at Otter Creek, Cocke found Boone and his men, and on relating his adventures, "came in for his share of applause." Boone at once despatched the master woodman, Michael Stoner, with pack-horses to assist Henderson's party, which he met on April 18th at their encampment "in the Eye of the Rich Land." Along with "Excellent Beef in plenty," Stoner brought the story of Boone's determined stand and an account of the erection of a rude little fortification which they had hurriedly thrown up to resist attack. With laconic significance Henderson pays the following tribute to Boone which deserves to be perpetuated in national annals: "It was owing to Boone's confidence in us, and the people's in him, that a stand was ever attempted in order to wait for our coming."

In the course of their journey over the mountains and through the wilderness, the pioneers forgot the trials of the trail in the face of the surpassing beauties of the country. The Cumberlands were covered with rich undergrowth of the red and white rhododendron, the delicate laurel, the mountain ivy, the flameazalea, the spicewood, and the cane; while the white stars of the dogwood and the carmine blossoms of the red-bud, strewn across the verdant background of the forest, gleamed in the eager air of spring. "To enter upon a detail of the Beuty & Goodness of our Country," writes Nathaniel Henderson, "would be a task too arduous . . . . Let it suffice to tell you it far exceeds any country I ever saw or herd off. I am conscious its out of the power of any man to make you clearly sensible of the great Beuty and Richness of Kentucky." Young Felix Walker, endowed with more vivid powers of description, says with a touch of native eloquence:

"Perhaps no Adventurer Since the days of donquicksotte or before ever felt So Cheerful & Ilated in prospect, every heart abounded with Joy & excitement . . . & exclusive of the Novelties of the Journey the advantages & accumalations arising on the Settlement of a new Country was a dazzling object with many of our Company . . . . As the Cain ceased, we began to discover the pleasing & Rapturous appearance of the plains of Kentucky, a New Sky & Strange Earth to be presented to our view . . . . So Rich a Soil we had never Saw before, Covered with Clover in full Bloom. the Woods alive abounding in wild Game, turkeys so numerous that it might be said there appeared but one flock Universally Scattered in the woods . . . it appeared that Nature in the profusion of her Bounties, had Spread a feast for all that lives, both for the Animal & Rational World, a Sight so delightful to our View and grateful to our feelings almost Induced us, in Immitation of Columbus in Transport to Kiss the Soil of Kentucky, as he haild & Saluted the sand on his first setting his foot on the Shores of America."

On the journey Henderson was joined in Powell's Valley by Benjamin Logan, afterward so famous in Kentucky annals, and a companion, William Galaspy. At the Crab Orchard they left Henderson's party; and turning their course westward finally pitched camp in the present Lincoln County, where Logan subsequently built a fort.

On Sunday, April 16th, on Scaggs's Creek, Henderson records: "About 12 oClock Met James McAfee with 18 other persons Returning from Cantucky." They advised Henderson of the "troublesomeness and danger" of the Indians, says Robert McAfee junior: "but Henderson assured them that he had purchased the whole country from the Indians, that it belonged to him, and he had named it Transylvania . . . . Robt, Samuel, and William McAfee and 3 others were inclined to return, but James opposed it, alleging that Henderson had no right to the land, and that Virginia had previously bought it. The former (6) returned with Henderson to Boonesborough."
Among those who had joined Henderson's party was Abraham Hanks from Virginia, the maternal grandfather of Abraham Lincoln; but alarmed by the stories brought by Stewart and his party of fugitives, Hanks and Drake, as recorded by William Calk on that day (April 13th), turned back.

At last the founder of Kentucky with his little band reached the destined goal of their arduous journeyings. Henderson's record on his birthday runs: "Thursday the 20th [April] Arrived at Fort Boone on the Mouth of Oter Creek Cantuckey River where we were Saluted by a running fire of about 25 Guns; all that was then at Fort . . . . The men appeared in high spirits & much rejoiced in our arrival." It is a coincidence of historic interest that just one day after the embattled farmers at Lexington and Concord "fired the shots heard round the world," the echoing shots of Boone and his sturdy backwoodsmen rang out to announce the arrival of the proprietor of Transylvania and the birth of the American West.

CHAPTER XV. Transylvania—A wilderness Commonwealth

You are about a work of the utmost importance to the well-being of this country in general, in which the interest and security of each and every individual are inseparably connected .... Our peculiar circumstances in this remote country, surrounded on all sides with difficulties, and equally subject to one common danger, which threatens our common overthrow, must, I think, in their effects, secure to us an union of interests, and, consequently, that harmony in opinion, so essential to the forming good, wise and wholesome laws.—Judge Richard Henderson: Address to the Legislature of Transylvania, May 23, 1775.

The independent spirit displayed by the Transylvania Company, and Henderson's procedure in open defiance of the royal governors of both North Carolina and Virginia, naturally aroused grave alarm throughout these colonies and South Carolina. "This in my Opinion," says Preston in a letter to George Washington (January 31, 1775), "will soon become a serious Affair, & highly deserves the Attention of the Government. For it is certain that a vast Number of People are preparing to go out and settle on this Purchase; and if once they get fixed there, it will be next to impossible to remove them or reduce them to Obedience; as they are so far from the Seat of Government. Indeed it may be the Cherokees will support them." Governor Martin of North Carolina, already deeply disturbed in anticipation of the coming revolutionary cataclysm, thundered in what was generally regarded as a forcible-feeble proclamation (February 19, 1775) against "Richard Henderson and his Confederates" in their "daring, unjust and unwarrantable proceedings." In a letter to Dartmouth he denounces "Henderson the famous invader" and dubs the Transylvania Company "an infamous Company of land Pyrates."

Officials who were themselves eager for land naturally opposed Henderson's plans. Lord Dunmore, who in 1774, as we have seen, was heavily interested in the Wabash Land Company engineered by William Murray, took the ground that the Wabash purchase was valid under the Camden-Yorke decision. This is so stated in the records of the Illinois Company. Likewise under Murray's control. But although the "Ouabache Company," of which Dunmore was a leading member, was initiated as early as May 16, 1774, the purchase of the territory was not formally effected until October 18, 1775—too late to benefit Dunmore, then deeply embroiled in the preliminaries to the Revolution. Under the cover of his agent's name, it is believed, Dunmore, with his "passion for land and fees," illegally entered tracts aggregating thousands of acres of land surveyed by the royal surveyors in the summer of 1774 for Dr. John Connolly. Early in this same year, Patrick Henry, who, as already pointed out, had entered large tracts in Kentucky in violation of Virginia's treaty obligations with the Cherokees, united with William Byrd 3d, John Page, Ralph Wormley, Samuel Overton, and William Christian, in the effort to purchase from the Cherokees a tract of land west of Donelson's line, being firmly persuaded of the validity of the Camden-Yorke opinion. Their agent, William Kenedy, considerably later in the year, went on a mission to the Cherokee towns, and upon his return reported that the Indians might be induced to sell. When it became known that Judge Henderson had organized the Transylvania Company and anticipated Patrick Henry and his associates, Colonel Arthur Campbell, as he himself states, applied to several of the partners of the Transylvania Company on behalf of Patrick Henry, requesting that Henry be taken in as a partner. It was afterward stated, as commonly understood among the Transylvania proprietors, that both Patrick Henry and Thomas Jefferson desired to become members of the company; but that Colonel Richard Henderson was instrumental in preventing their admission "lest they should supplant the Colonel [Henderson] as the guiding spirit of the company."

Fully informed by Preston's elaborate communication on the gravity of the situation, Dunmore acted energetically, though tardily, to prevent the execution of Henderson's designs. On March 21st Dunmore sent flying through the back country a proclamation, demanding the immediate relinquishment of the territory by "one Richard Henderson and other disorderly persons, his associates," and "in case of refusal, and of violently detaining such possession, that he or they be immediately fined and imprisoned. This proclamation, says a peppery old chronicler, may well rank with the one excepting those arch traitors and rebels, Samuel Adams and John Hancock, from the mercy of the British monarch. In view of Dunmore's confidence in the validity of the Camden-Yorke decision, it is noteworthy that no mention of the royal proclamation of 1763 occurs in his broadside; and that he bases his objection to the Transylvania purchase upon the king's instructions that all vacant lands "within this colony" be laid off in tracts, from one hundred to one thousand acres in extent, and sold at public auction. This proclamation which was enclosed, oddly enough, in a letter of official instructions to Preston warning him not to survey any lands "beyond the line run by Colonel Donaldson," proved utterly ineffective. At the same time, Dunmore despatched a pointed letter to Oconostota, Atta-kulla-kulla, Judge's Friend, and other Cherokee chieftains, notifying them that the sale of the great tract of land below the Kentucky was illegal and threatening them with the king's displeasure if they did not repudiate the sale.

News of the plans which Henderson had already matured for establishing an independent colony in the trans-Alleghany wilderness, now ran like wild-fire through Virginia. In a letter to George Washington (April 9, 1775), Preston ruefully says: "Henderson I hear has made the Purchase & got a Conveyance of the great and Valluable Country below the Kentucky from the Cherokees. He and about 300 adventurers are gone out to take Possession, who it is said intends to set up an independent Government & form a Code of Laws for themselves. How this may be I cant say, but I am affraid the steps taken by the Government have been too late. Before the Purchase was made had the Governor interfered it is believed the Indians would not have sold."

Meanwhile Judge Henderson, with strenuous energy, had begun to erect a large stockaded fort according to plans of his own. Captain James Harrod with forty-two men was stationed at the settlement he had made the preceding year, having arrived there before the McAfees started back to Virginia; and there were small groups of settlers at Boiling Spring, six miles southeast of Harrods settlement, and at St. Asaph's, a mile west of the present Stanford. A representative government for Transylvania was then planned. When the frank and gallant Floyd arrived at the

Transylvania Fort on May 3d, he "expressed great satisfaction," says Judge Henderson, "on being informed of the plan we proposed for Legislation & sayd he must most heartily concur in that & every other measure we should adopt for the well Govern'g or good of the Community in Gen'l." In reference to a conversation with Captain James Harrod and Colonel Thomas Slaughter of Virginia, Henderson notes in his diary (May 8th): "Our plan of Legislation, the evils pointed out—the remedies to be applyed &c &c &c were Acceeded to without Hesitation. The plann was plain & Simple--'twas nothing novel in its essence a thousand years ago it was in use, and found by every year's experience since to be unexceptionable. We were in four distinct settlem'ts. Members or delegates from every place by free choice of Individuals they first having entered into writings solemnly binding themselves to obey and carry into Execution Such Laws as representatives should from time to time make, Concurred with, by A Majority of the Proprietors present in the Country."

In reply to inquiries of the settlers, Judge Henderson gave as his reason for this assembling of a Transylvania Legislature that "all power was derived from the people." Six days before the prophetic arrival of the news of the Battle of Lexington and eight days before the revolutionary committee of Mecklenburg County, North Carolina, promulgated their memorable Resolves establishing laws for independent government, the pioneers assembled on the green beneath the mighty plane-tree at the Transylvania Fort. In his wise and statesmanlike address to this picturesque convention of free Americans (May 23, 1775), an address which Felix Walker described as being "considered equal to any of like kind ever delivered to any deliberate body in that day and time," Judge Henderson used these memorable words:

"You, perhaps, are fixing the palladium, or placing the first corner stone of an edifice, the height and magnificence of whose superstructure . . . can only become great in proportion to the excellence of its foundation . . . . If any doubt remain amongst you with respect to the force or efficiency of whatever laws you now, or hereafter make, be pleased to consider that *all power is originally in the people; make and their interest, therefore, by impartial and beneficent laws, and you may be sure of their inclination to see them enforced.*"

An early writer, in speaking of the full blooded democracy of these "advanced" sentiments, quaintly comments: "If Jeremy Bentham had been in existence of manhood, he would have sent his compliments to the President of Transylvania." This, the first representative body of American freemen which ever convened west of the Alleghanies, is surely the most unique colonial government ever set up on this continent. The proceedings of this backwoods legislature—the democratic leader ship of the principal proprietor; the prudence exhibited in the laws for protecting game, breeding horses, *etc.*; the tolerance shown in the granting of full religious liberty—all display the acumen and practical wisdom of these pioneer law-givers. As the result of Henderson's tactfulness, the proprietary form of government, thoroughly democratized in tone, was complacently accepted by the backwoods men. From one who, though still under royal rule, vehemently asserted that the source of all political power was the people, and that "laws derive force and efficiency from our mutual consent," Western democracy thus born in the wilderness was "taking its first political lesson." In their answer to Henderson's assertion of freedom from alien authority the pioneers unhesitatingly declared: "That we have an absolute right, as a political body, without giving umbrage to Great Britain, or any of the colonies, to form rules for the government of our little society, cannot be doubted by any sensible mind and being without the jurisdiction of, and not answerable to any of his Majesty's courts, the constituting tribunals of justice shall be a matter of our first contemplation . . . ." In the establishment of a constitution for the new colony, Henderson with paternalistic wisdom induced the people to adopt a legal code based on the laws of England. Out of a sense of self-protection he reserved for the proprietors only one prerogative not granted them by the people, the right of veto. He clearly realized that if this power were given up, the delegates to any convention that might be held after the first would be able to assume the claims and rights of the proprietors.

A land-office was formally opened, deeds were issued, and a store was established which supplied the colonists with powder, lead, salt, osnaburgs, blankets, and other chief necessities of pioneer existence. Writing to his brother Jonathan from Leestown, the bold young George Rogers Clark, soon to plot the downfall of Transylvania, enthusiastically says (July 6, 1775): "A richer and more Beautifull Cuntry than this I believe has never been seen in America yet. Col. Henderson is hear and Claims all ye Country below Kentucke. If his Claim Should be good, land may be got Reasonable Enough and as good as any in ye World." Those who settled on the south side of Kentucky River acknowledged the validity of the Transylvania purchase; and Clark in his Memoir says: "the Proprietors at first took great pains to Ingratiate themselves in the fav'r of the people."

In regard to the designs of Lord Dunmore, who, as noted above, had illegally entered the Connolly grant on the Ohio and sought to outlaw Henderson, and of Colonel William Byrd 3d, who, after being balked in Patrick Henry's plan to anticipate the Transylvania Company in effecting a purchase from the Cherokees, was supposed to have tried to persuade the Cherokees to repudiate the "Great Treaty," Henderson defiantly says: "Whether Lord Dunmore and Colonel Byrd have interfered with the Indians or not, Richard Henderson is equally ignorant and indifferent. The utmost result of their efforts can only serve to convince them of the futility of their schemes and possibly frighten some few faint-hearted persons, naturally prone to reverence great names and fancy everything must shrink at the magic of a splendid title."

Prompted by Henderson's desire to petition the Continental Congress then in session for recognition as the fourteenth colony, the Transylvania legislature met again on the first Thursday in September and elected Richard Henderson and John Williams, among others, as delegates to the gathering at Philadelphia. Shortly afterward the Proprietors of Transylvania held a meeting at Oxford, North Carolina (September 25, 1775), elected Williams as the agent of the colony, and directed him to proceed to Boonesborough there to reside until April, 1776. James Hogg, of Hillsborough, chosen as Delegate to represent the Colony in the Continental Congress, was despatched to Philadelphia, bearing with him an elaborate memorial prepared by the President, Judge Henderson, petitioning the Congress "to take the infant Colony of Transylvania into their protection."

Almost immediately upon his arrival in Philadelphia, James Hogg was presented to "the famous Samuel and John Adams." The latter warned Hogg, in view of the efforts then making toward reconciliation between the colonies and the king, that "the taking under our protection a body of people who have acted in defiance of the King's proclamation, will be looked on as a confirmation of that independent spirit with which we are daily reproached." Jefferson said that if his advice were followed, all the use the Virginians should make of their charter would be "to prevent any arbitrary or oppressive government to be established within the boundaries of it"; and that it was his wish "to see a free government established at the back of theirs [Virginia's] properly united with them." He would not consent, however, that Congress should acknowledge the colony of Transylvania, until it had the approbation of the Virginia Convention. The quit-rents imposed by the company were denounced in Congress as a mark of vassalage; and many advised a law against the employment of negroes in the colony. "They even threatened us with their opposition," says Hogg, with precise veracity, "if we do not act upon liberal principles when we have it so much in our power to render ourselves immortal."

CHAPTER XVI. The Repulse of the Red Men

To this short war may be properly attributed all the kind feelings and fidelity to treaty stipulations manifested by the Cherokees ever afterwards. General Rutherford instilled into the Indians so great a fear of the whites, that never afterwards were they disposed to engage in any cruelty, or destroy any of the property of our frontier men.—David L. Swain: The Indian War of 1776.

During the summer of 1775 the proprietors of Transylvania were confronted with two stupendous tasks—that of winning the favor and support of the frontiersmen and that of rallying the rapidly dwindling forces in Kentucky in defense of the settlements. Recognizing the difficulty of including Martin's Station, because of its remoteness, with the government provided for Transylvania, Judge Henderson prepared a plan of government for the group of settlers located in Powell's Valley. In a letter to Martin (July 30th), in regard to the recent energetic defense of the settlers at that point against the Indians, Henderson says: "Your spirited conduct gives me much pleasure . . . . Keep your men in heart if possible, *now is our time, the Indians must not drive us.*" The gloom which had been occasioned by the almost complete desertion of the stations at Harrodsburg, the Boiling Spring, and the Transylvania Fort or Boonesborough was dispelled with the return of Boone, accompanied by some thirty persons, on September 8th, and of Richard Callaway with a considerable party on September 26th. The crisis was now passed; and the colony began for the first time really to flourish. The people on the south side of the Kentucky River universally accepted proprietary rule for the time being. But the seeds of dissension were soon to be sown among those who settled north of the river, as well as among men of the stamp of James Harrod, who, having preceded Henderson in the establishment of a settlement in Kentucky, naturally resented holding lands under the Transylvania Company.

The great liberality of this organization toward incoming settlers had resulted in immense quantities of land being taken up through their land-office. The ranging, hunting, and road-building were paid for by the company; and the entire settlement was furnished with powder, lead, and supplies, wholly on credit, for this and the succeeding year. "Five hundred and sixty thousand acres of land are now entered," reports Floyd on December 1st, "and most of the people waiting to have it run out." After Dunmore, having lost his hold upon the situation, escaped to the protection of a British vessel, the Fowey, Colonel Preston continued to prevent surveys for officers' grants within the Transylvania territory; and his original hostility to Judge Henderson gave place to friendship and support. On December 1st, Colonel John Williams, resident agent of the Transylvania Company, announced at Boonesborough the long-contemplated and widely advertised advance in price of the lands, from twenty to fifty shillings per hundred acres, with surveying fees of four dollars for tracts not exceeding six hundred and forty acres. At a meeting of the Transylvania legislature, convened on December 21st, John Floyd was chosen surveyor general of the colony, Nathaniel Henderson was placed in charge of the Entering Office, and Richard Harrison given the post of secretary. At this meeting of the legislature, the first open expression of discontent was voiced in the "Harrodsburg Remonstrance," questioning the validity of the proprietors' title, and protesting against any increase in the price of lands, as well as the taking up by the proprietors and a few other gentlemen of the best lands at the Falls of the Ohio. Every effort was made to accommodate the remonstrants, who were led by Abraham Hite. Office fees were abolished, and the payment of quit-rents was deferred until January 1, 1780. Despite these efforts at accommodation, grave doubts were implanted by this Harrodsburg Remonstrance in the minds of the people; and much discussion and discontent ensued.

By midsummer, 1775, George Rogers Clark, a remarkably enterprising and independent young pioneer, was "engrossing all the land he could" in Kentucky. Upon his return to Virginia, as he relates, he "found there was various oppinions Respecting Henderson claim. many thought it good, others douted whether or not Virginia coud with propriety have any pretentions to the cuntrey." Jefferson displayed a liberal attitude toward the claims of the Transylvania proprietors; and Patrick Henry openly stated that, in his opinion, "their claim would stand good." But many others, of the stamp of George Mason and George Washington, vigorously asserted Virginia's charter rights over the Western territory." This sharp difference of opinion excited in Clark's mind the bold conception of seizing the leadership of the country and making terms with Virginia under threat of secession. With the design of effecting some final disposition in regard to the title of the Transylvania proprietors, Judge Henderson and Colonel Williams set off from Boonesborough about May 1st, intending first to appeal to the Virginia Convention and ultimately to lay their claims before the Continental Congress. "Since they have gone," reports Floyd to Preston, "I am told most of the men about Harrodsburg have re-assumed their former resolution of not complying with any of the office rules whatever. Jack Jones, it is said, is at the head of the party & flourishes away prodigiously." John Gabriel Jones was the mere figurehead in the revolt. The real leader, the brains of the conspiracy, was the unscrupulous George Rogers Clark. At Clark's instance, an eight-day election was held at Harrodsburg (June 7-15), at which time a petition to the Virginia Convention was drawn up; and Clark and Jones were elected delegates. Clark's plan, the scheme of a bold revolutionist, was to treat with Virginia for terms; and if they were not satisfactory, to revolt and, as he says, "Establish an Independent Government" . . . "giving away great part of the Lands and disposing of the Remainder." In a second petition, prepared by the self-styled "Committee of West Fincastle" (June 20th), it was alleged that "if these pretended Proprietors have leave to continue to act in their arbitrary manner out the controul of this colony [Virginia] the end must be evident to every well wisher to American Liberty."

The contest which now ensued between Richard Henderson and George Rogers Clark, waged upon the floor of the convention and behind the scenes, resulted in a conclusion that was inevitable at a moment in American history marked by the signing of the Declaration of Independence. Virginia, under the leader ship of her new governor, Patrick Henry, put an end to the proprietary rule of the Transylvania Company. On December 7th such part of Transylvania as lay within the chartered limits of Virginia was erected by the legislature of that colony into the County of Kentucky. The proprietary form of government with its "marks of vassalage," although liberalized with the spirit of democracy, was unendurable to the independent and lawless pioneers, already intoxicated with the spirit of freedom swept in on the first fresh breezes of the Revolution. Yet it is not to be doubted that the Transylvania Company, through the courage and moral influence of its leaders, made a permanent contribution to the colonization of the West, which, in providential timeliness and effective execution, is without parallel in our early annals.

While events were thus shaping themselves in Kentucky—events which made possible Clark's spectacular and meteoric campaign in the Northwest and ultimately resulted in the establishment of the Mississippi instead of the Alleghanies as the western boundary of the Confederation—the pioneers of Watauga were sagaciously laying strong the foundations of permanent occupation. In September, 1775, North Carolina, through her Provincial Congress, provided for the appointment in each district of a Committee of Safety, to consist of a president and twelve other members. Following the lead thus set, the Watauga settlers assumed for their country the name of "Washington District"; and proceeded by unanimous vote of the people to choose a committee of thirteen, which included James Robertson and John Sevier. This district was organized "shortly after October, 1775, according to Felix Walker; and the first step taken after the election of the committee was the organization of a court, consisting of five members. Felix Walker was elected clerk of the court thus organized, and held the position for about four years. James Robertson and John Sevier, it is believed, were also members of this court. To James Robertson who, with the assistance of his colleagues, devised this primitive type of frontier rule—a true commission form of government, on the "Watauga Plan"—is justly due distinctive recognition for this notable inauguration of the independent democracy of the Old Southwest. The Watauga settlement was animated by a spirit of deepest loyalty to the American cause. In a memorable petition these hardy settlers requested the Provincial Council of North Carolina not to regard them as a "lawless mob," but to "annex" them to North Carolina without delay. "This committee (willing to become a party in the present unhappy contest)", states the petition, which must have been drafted about July 15, 1776, "resolved (which is now on our records), to adhere strictly to the rules and orders of the Continental Congress, and in open committee acknowledged themselves indebted to the united colonies their full proportion of the Continental expense."

While these disputes as to the government of the new communities were in progress an additional danger threatened the pioneers. For a whole year the British had been plying the various Indian tribes from the lakes to the gulf with presents, supplies, and ammunition. In the Northwest bounties had actually been offered for American scalps. During the spring of 1776 plans were concerted, chiefly through Stuart and Cameron, British agents among the Southern Indians, for uniting the Loyalists and the Indians in a crushing attack upon the Tennessee settlements and the back country of North Carolina. Already the frontier of South Carolina had passed through the horrors of Indian uprising; and warning of the approaching invasion had been mercifully sent the Holston settlers by Atta-kulla-kulla's niece, Nancy Ward, the "Pocahontas of the West"—doubtless through the influence of her daughter, who loved Joseph Martin. The settlers, flocking for refuge into their small stockaded forts, waited in readiness for the dreaded Indian attacks, which were made by two forces totaling some seven hundred warriors.

On July 20th, warned in advance of the approach of the Indians, the borderers, one hundred and seventy in all, marched in two columns from the rude breastwork, hastily thrown up at Eaton's Station, to meet the Indians, double their own number, led by The Dragging Canoe. The scouts surprised one party of Indians, hastily poured in a deadly fire, and rushed upon them with such impetuous fury that they fled precipitately. Withdrawing now toward their breastwork, in anticipation of encountering there a larger force, the backwoodsmen suddenly found themselves attacked in their rear and in grave danger of being surrounded. Extending their own line under the direction of Captain James Shelby, the frontiersmen steadily met the bold attack of the Indians, who, mistaking the rapid extension of the line for a movement to retreat, incautiously made a headlong onslaught upon the whites, giving the war-whoop and shouting: "The Unakas are running!" In the ensuing hot conflict at close quarters, in some places hand to hand, the Indians were utterly routed—The Dragging Canoe being shot down, many warriors wounded, and thirteen left dead upon the field.

On the day after Thompson, Cocke, Shelby, Campbell, Madison, and their men were thus winning the battle of the Long Island "flats," Robertson, Sevier, and their little band of forty-two men were engaged in repelling an attack, begun at sunrise, upon the Watauga fort near the Sycamore Shoals. This attack, which was led by Old Abraham, proved abortive; but as the result of the loose investment of the log fortress, maintained by the Indians for several weeks, a few rash venturers from the fort were killed or captured, notably a young boy who was carried to one of the Indian towns and burned at the stake, and the wife of the pioneer settler, William Been, who was rescued from a like fate by the intercession of the humane and noble Nancy Ward. It was during this siege, according to constant tradition, that a frontier lass, active and graceful as a young doe, was pursued to the very stockade by the fleet-footed savages. Seeing her plight, an athletic young officer mounted the stockade at a single leap, shot down the foremost of the pursuers, and leaning over, seized the maiden by the hands and lifted her over the stockade. The maiden who sank breathless into the arms of the young officer, John Sevier, was "Bonnie Kate Sherrill"—who, after the fashion of true romance, afterward became the wife of her gallant rescuer.

While the Tennessee settlements were undergoing the trials of siege and attack, the settlers on the frontiers of Rowan were falling beneath the tomahawk of the merciless savage. In the first and second weeks of July large forces of Indians penetrated to the outlying settlements; and in two days thirty-seven persons were killed along the Catawba River. On July 13th, the bluff old soldier of Rowan, General Griffith Rutherford, reported to the council of North Carolina that "three of our Captains are killed and one wounded"; and that he was setting out that day with what men he could muster to relieve Colonel McDowell, ten men, and one hundred and twenty women and children, who were "besieged in some kind of a fort." Aroused to extraordinary exertions by these daring and deadly blows, the governments of North Carolina, South Carolina, Virginia, and Georgia instituted a joint campaign against the Cherokees. It was believed that, by delivering a series of crushing blows to the Indians and so conclusively demonstrating the overwhelming superiority of the whites, the state governments in the Old Southwest would convince the savages of the futility, of any attempt ever again to oppose them seriously.

Within less than a week after sending his despatches to the council Rutherford set forth at the head of twenty-five hundred men to protect the frontiers of North Carolina and to overwhelm the foe. Leading the South Carolina army of more than eighteen hundred men, Colonel Andrew Williamson directed his attack against the lower Cherokee towns; while Colonel Samuel Jack led two hundred Georgians against the Indian towns at the heads of the Chattahoochee and Tugaloo Rivers. Assembling a force of some sixteen hundred Virginians, Colonel William Christian rendezvoused in August at the Long Island of Holston, where his force was strengthened by between three and four hundred North Carolinians under Colonels Joseph Williams and Love, and Major Winston. The various expeditions met with little effective opposition on the whole, succeeding everywhere in their design of utterly laying waste the towns of the Cherokees. One serious engagement occurred when the Indians resolutely challenged Rutherford's advance at the gap of the Nantahala Mountains. Indian women—heroic Amazons disguised in war-paint and armed with the weapons of warriors and the courage of despair—fought side by side with the Indian braves in the effort to arrest Rutherford's progress and compass his defeat. More than forty frontiersmen fell beneath the deadly shots of this truly Spartan band before the final repulse of the savages.

The most picturesque figures in this overwhelmingly successful campaign were the bluff old Indian-fighter, Griffith Rutherford, wearing "a tow hunting shirt, dyed black, and trimmed with white fringe" as a uniform; Captain Benjamin Cleveland, a rude paladin of gigantic size, strength, and courage; Lieutenant William Lenoir (Le Noir), the gallant and recklessly brave French Huguenot, later to win a general's rank in the Revolution; and that militant man of God, the Reverend James Hall, graduate of Nassau Hall, stalwart and manly, who carried a rifle on his shoulder and, in the intervals between the slaughter of the savages, preached the gospel to the vindictive and bloodthirsty backwoodsmen. Such preaching was sorely needed on that campaign— when the whites, maddened beyond the bounds of self-control by the recent ghastly murders, gladly availed themselves of the South Carolina bounty offered for fresh Indian scalps. At times they exultantly displayed the reeking patches of hair above the gates of their stockades; at others, with many a bloody oath, they compelled their commanders either to sell the Indian captives into slavery or else see them scalped on the spot. Twenty years afterward Benjamin Hawkins relates that among Indian refugees in extreme western Georgia the children had been so terrorized by their parents' recitals of the atrocities of the enraged borderers in the campaign of 1776, that they ran screaming from the face of a white man.

CHAPTER XVII. The Colonization of the Cumberland

March 31, 1760. Set out this day, and after running some distance, met with Col. Richard Henderson, who was running the line between Virginia and North Carolina. At this meeting we were much rejoiced. He gave us every information we wished, and further informed us that he had purchased a quantity of corn in Kentucky, to be shipped at the Falls of Ohio, for the use of the Cumberland settlement. We are now without bread, and are compelled to hunt the buffalo to preserve life.—John Donelson: Journal of a Voyage, intended by God's permission, in the good boat Adventure, from Fort Patrick Henry, on Holston River, to the French Salt Springs on Cumberland River.

To the settlements in Tennessee and Kentucky, which they had seized and occupied, the pioneers held on with a tenacious grip which never relaxed. From these strongholds, won through sullen and desperate strokes, they pushed deeper into the wilderness, once again to meet with undimmed courage the bitter onslaughts of their resentful foes. The crushing of the Cherokees in 1776 relieved the pressure upon the Tennessee settlers, enabling them to strengthen their hold and prepare effectively for future eventualities; the possession of the gateway to Kentucky kept free the passage for Western settlement; Watauga and its defenders continued to offer a formidable barrier to British invasion of the East from Kentucky and the Northwest during the Revolution; while these Tennessee frontiersmen were destined soon to set forth again to invade a new wilderness and at frightful cost to colonize the Cumberland.

The little chain of stockades along the farflung frontier of Kentucky was tenaciously held by the bravest of the race, grimly resolved that this chain must not break. The Revolution precipitated against this chain wave after wave of formidable Indian foes from the Northwest under British leadership. At the very time when Grifth Rutherford set out for the relief of McDowell's Fort, a marauding Indian band captured by stealth near the Transylvania Fort, known as Boone's Fort (Boonesborough), Elizabeth and Frances Callaway, and Jemima Boone, the daughters of Richard Callaway and Daniel Boone, and rapidly marched them away toward the Shawanoe towns on the Ohio. A relief party, in two divisions, headed respectively by the young girls' fathers, and composed among others of the lovers of the three girls, Samuel Henderson, John Holder, and Flanders Callaway, pursued them with almost incredible swiftness. Guided by broken twigs and bits of cloth surreptitiously dropped by Elizabeth Callaway, they finally overtook the unsuspecting savages, killed two of them, and rescued the three maidens unharmed. This romantic episode—which gave Fenimore Cooper the theme for the most memorable scene in one of his Leatherstocking Tales had an even more romantic sequel in the subsequent marriage of the three pairs of lovers.

This bold foray, so shrewdly executed and even more sagaciously foiled, was a true precursor of the dread happenings of the coming neighborhood of the stations; and relief was felt when the Transylvania Fort, the great stockade planned by Judge Henderson, was completed by the pioneers (July, 1776). Glad tidings arrived only a few days later when the Declaration of Independence, read aloud from the Virginia

Gazette, was greeted with wild huzzas by the patriotic backwoodsmen. During the ensuing months occasional invasions were made by savage bands; but it was not until April 24, 1777, that Henderson's "big fort" received its first attack, being invested by a company of some seventy-five savages. The twenty-two riflemen in the fort drove off the painted warriors, but not before Michael Stoner, Daniel Boone, and several others were severely wounded. As he lay helpless upon the ground, his ankle shattered by a bullet, Boone was lifted by Simon Kenton and borne away upon his shoulders to the haven of the stockade amid a veritable shower of balls. The stoical and taciturn Boone clasped Kenton's hand and gave him the accolade of the wilderness in the brief but heartfelt utterance; "You are a fine fellow." On July 4th of this same year the fort was again subjected to siege, when two hundred gaudily painted savages surrounded it for two days. But owing to the vigilance and superb markmanship of the defenders, as well as to the lack of cannon by the besieging force, the Indians reluctantly abandoned the siege, after leaving a number dead upon the field. Soon afterward the arrival of two strong bodies of prime riflemen, who had been hastily summoned from the frontiers of North Carolina and Virginia, once again made firm the bulwark of white supremacy in the West.

Kentucky's terrible year, 1778, opened with a severe disaster to the white settlers—-when Boone with thirty men, while engaged in making salt at the "Lower Salt Spring," was captured in February by more than a hundred Indians, sent by Governor Hamilton of Detroit to drive the white settlers from "Kentucke." Boone remained in captivity until early summer, when, learning that his Indian captors were planning an attack in force upon the Transylvania Fort, he succeeded in effecting his escape. After a break-neck journey of one hundred and sixty miles, during which he ate but one meal, Boone finally arrived at the big fort on June 20th. The settlers were thus given ample time for preparation, as the long siege did not begin until September 7th. The fort was invested by a powerful force flying the English flag—four hundred and forty-four savages gaudy in the vermilion and ochre of their war-paint, and eleven Frenchmen, the whole being commanded by the French-Canadian, Captain Dagniaux de Quindre, and the great Indian Chief, Black-fish who had adopted Boone as a son. In the effort to gain his end de Quindre resorted to a dishonorable stratagem, by which he hoped to outwit the settlers and capture the fort with but slight loss. "They formed a scheme to deceive us," says Boone, "declaring it was their orders, from Governor Hamilton, to take us captives, and not to destroy us; but if nine of us would come out and treat with them, they would immediately withdraw their forces from our walls, and return home peacably." Transparent as the stratagem was, Boone incautiously agreed to a conference with the enemy; Callaway alone took the precaution to guard against Indian duplicity. After a long talk, the Indians proposed to Boone, Callaway, and the seven or eight pioneers who accompanied them that they shake hands in token of peace and friendship. As picturesquely described by Daniel Trabue:

"The Indians sayed two Indians must shake hands with one white man to make a Double or sure peace at this time the Indians had hold of the white men's hands and held them. Col. Calloway objected to this but the other Indians laid hold or tryed to lay hold of the other hand but Colonel Calloway was the first that jerked away from them but the Indians seized the men two Indians holt of one man or it was mostly the case and did their best to hold them but while the man and Indians was a scuffling the men from the Fort agreeable to Col. Calloway's order fired on them they had a dreadful skuffel but our men all got in the fort safe and the fire continued on both sides."

During the siege Callaway, the leader of the pioneers, made a wooden cannon wrapped with wagon tires, which on being fired at a group of Indians "made them scamper perdidiously." The secret effort of the Indians to tunnel a way underground into the fort, being discovered by the defenders, was frustrated by a countermine. Unable to outwit, outfight, or outmaneuver the resourceful Callaway, de Quindre finally withdrew on September 16th, closing the longest and severest attack that any of the fortified stations of Kentucky had ever been called upon to withstand.

The successful defense of the Transylvania Fort, made by these indomitable backwoodsmen who were lost sight of by the Continental Congress and left to fight alone their battles in the forests, was of national significance in its results. Had the Transylvania Fort fallen, the northern Indians in overwhelming numbers, directed by Hamilton and led by British officers, might well have swept Kentucky free of defenders and fallen with devastating force upon the exposed settlements along the western frontiers of North Carolina, Virginia, and Pennsylvania, This defense of Boonesborough, therefore, is deserving of commemoration in the annals of the Revolution, along with Lexington and Bunker's Hill. Coupled with Clark's meteoric campaign in the Northwest and the subsequent struggles in the defense of Kentucky, it may be regarded as an event basically responsible for the retention of the trans-Alleghany region by the United States. The bitter struggles, desperate sieges, and bloody reprisals of these dark years came to a close with the expeditions of Clark and Logan in November, 1782, which appropriately concluded the Revolution in the West by putting a definite end to all prospect of formidable invasion of Kentucky.

In November, 1777, "Washington District," the delegates of which had been received in the preceding year by the Provincial Congress of North Carolina, was formed by the North Carolina General Assembly into Washington County; and to it were assigned the boundaries of the whole of the present state of Tennessee. While this immense territory was thus being definitely included within the bounds of North Carolina, Judge Henderson on behalf of the Transylvania Company was making a vigorous effort to secure the reestablishment of its rights from the Virginia Assembly. By order of the Virginia legislature, an exhaustive investigation of the claims of the Transylvania Company was therefore made, hearings being held at various points in the back country. On July 18, 1777, Judge Henderson presented to the peace commissioners for North Carolina and Virginia at the Long Island treaty ground an elaborate memorial in behalf of the Transylvania Company, which the commissioners unanimously refused to consider, as not coming under their jurisdiction. Finally, after a full and impartial discussion before the Virginia House of Delegates, that body declared the Transylvania purchase void. But in consideration of "the very great expense [incurred by the company] in making the said purchase, and in settling the said lands, by which the commonwealth is likely to receive great advantage, by increasing its inhabitants, and establishing a barrier against the Indians," the House of Delegates granted Richard Henderson and Company two hundred thousand acres of land situated between the Ohio and Green rivers, where the town of Henderson, Kentucky, now stands. With this bursting of the Transylvania bubble and the vanishing of the golden dreams of Henderson and his associates for establishing the fourteenth American colony in the heart of the trans-Alleghany, a first romantic chapter in the history of Westward expansion comes to a close.

But another and more feasible project immediately succeeded. Undiscouraged by Virginia's confiscation of Transylvania, and disregarding North Carolina's action in extending her boundaries over the trans-Alleghany region lying within her chartered limits, Henderson, in whom the genius of the colonizer and the ambition of the speculative capitalist were found in striking conjunction, was now inspired to repeat, along broader and more solidly practical lines, the revolutionary experiment of Transylvania. It was not his purpose, however, to found an independent colony; for he believed that millions of acres in the Transylvania purchase lay within the bounds of North Carolina, and he wished to open for colonization, settlement, and the sale of lands, the vast wilderness of the valley of the Cumberland supposed to lie within those confines. But so universal was the prevailing uncertainty in regard to boundaries that it was necessary to prolong the North Carolina-Virginia line in order to determine whether or not the Great French Lick, the ideal location for settlement, lay within the chartered limits of North Carolina.

Judge Henderson's comprehensive plans for the promotion of an extensive colonization of the Cumberland region soon began to take form in vigorous action. Just as in his Transylvania project Henderson had chosen Daniel Boone, the ablest of the North Carolina pioneers, to spy out the land and select sites for future location, so now he chose as leader of the new colonizing party the ablest of the Tennessee pioneers, James Robertson. Although he was the acknowledged leader of the Watauga settlement and held the responsible position of Indian agent for North Carolina, Robertson was induced by Henderson's liberal offers to leave his comparatively peaceful home and to venture his life in this desperate hazard of new fortunes. The advance party of eight white men and one negro, under Robertson's leadership, set forth from the Holston settlement on February 6, 1779, to make a preliminary exploration and to plant corn "that bread might be prepared for the main body of emigrants in the fall." After erecting a few cabins for dwellings and posts of defense, Robertson plunged alone into the wilderness and made the long journey to Post St. Vincent in the Illinois, in order to consult with George Rogers Clark, who had entered for himself in the Virginia Land Office several thousand acres of land at the French Lick. After perfecting arrangements with Clark for securing "cabin rights" should the land prove to lie in Virginia, Robertson returned to Watauga to take command of the migration.

Toward the end of the year two parties set out, one by land, the other by water, for the wonderful new country on the Cumberland of which Boone and Scaggs and Mansker had brought back such glowing descriptions. During the autumn Judge Henderson and other commissioners from North Carolina, in conjunction with commissioners from Virginia, had been running out the boundary line between the two states. On the very day—Christmas, 1779—that Judge Henderson reached the site of the Transylvania Fort, now called Boonesborough, the swarm of colonists from the parent hive at Watauga, under Robertson's leadership, reached the French Lick and on New Year's Day, 1780, crossed the river on the ice to the present site of Nashville.

The journal of the other party, which, as has been aptly said, reads like a chapter from one of Captain Mayne Reid's fascinating novels of adventure, was written by Colonel John Donelson, the father-in-law of Andrew Jackson. Setting out from Fort Patrick Henry on Holston River, December 22, 1779, with a flotilla consisting of about thirty flatboats, dugouts, and canoes, they encountered few difficulties until they began to run the gauntlet of the Chickamauga towns on the Tennessee. Here they were furiously attacked by the Indians, terrible in their red and black war-paint; and a well-filled boat lagging in the rear, with smallpox on board, was driven to shore by the Indians. The occupants were massacred; but the Indians at once contracted the disease and died by the hundreds. This luckless sacrifice of "poor Stuart, his family and friends," while a ghastly price to pay, undoubtedly procured for the Cumberland settlements comparative immunity from Indian forays until the new-comers had firmly established themselves in their wilderness stronghold. Eloquent of the granite endurance and courageous spirit of the typical American pioneer in its thankfulness for sanctuary, for reunion of families and friends, and for the humble shelter of a log cabin, is the last entry in Donelson's diary (April 24, 1780):

"This day we arrived at our journey's end at the Big Salt Lick, where we have the pleasure of finding Capt. Robertson and his company. It is a source of satisfaction to us to be enabled to restore to him and others their families and friends, who were intrusted to our care, and who, some time since, perhaps, despaired of ever meeting again. Though our prospects at present are dreary, we have found a few log cabins which have been built on a cedar bluff above the Lick by Capt. Robertson and his company."

In the midst of the famine during this terrible period of the "hard winter," Judge Henderson was sorely concerned for the fate of the new colony which he had projected, and immediately proceeded to purchase at huge cost a large stock of corn. On March 5, 1780, this corn, which had been raised by Captain Nathaniel Hart, was "sent from Boonesborough in perogues [pettiaugers or flatboats] under the command of William Bailey Smith . . . . This corn was taken down the Kentucky River, and over the Falls of Ohio, to the mouth of the Cumberland, and thence up that river to the fort at the French Lick. It is believed have been the only bread which the settlers had until it was raised there in 1781." There is genuine impressiveness in this heroic triumphing over the obstacles of obdurate nature and this paternalistic provision for the exposed Cumberland settlement—the purchase by Judge Henderson, the shipment by Captain Hart, and the transportation by Colonel Smith, in an awful winter of bitter cold and obstructed navigation, of this indispensable quantity of corn purchased for sixty thousand dollars in depreciated currency.

Upon his arrival at the French Lick, shortly after the middle of April, Judge Henderson at once proceeded to organize a government for the little community. On May 1st articles of association were drawn up; and important additions thereto were made on May 13th, when the settlers signed the complete series. The original document, still preserved, was drafted by Judge Henderson, being written throughout in his own handwriting; and his name heads the list of two hundred and fifty and more signatures. The "Cumberland Compact," as this paper is called, is fundamentally a mutual contract between the copartners of the Transylvania Company and the settlers upon the lands claimed by the company. It represents the collective will of the community; and on account of the careful provisions safeguarding the rights of each party to the contract it may be called a bill of rights. The organization of this pure democracy was sound and admirable—another notable early example of the commission form of government. The most remarkable feature of this backwoods constitution marks Judge Henderson as a pioneer in the use of the political device so prominent to-day, one hundred and forty years later—the "recall of judges." In the following striking clause this innovation in government was recognized thus early in American history as the most effective means of securing and safeguarding justice in a democracy:

"As often as the people in general are dissatisfied with the doings of the Judges or Triers so to be chosen, they may call a new selection in any of the said stations, and elect bothers in their stead, having due respect to the number now agreed to be elected at each station, which persons so to be chosen shall have the same power with those in whose room or place they shall or may be chosen to act."

A land-office was now opened, the entry-taker being appointed by Judge Henderson, in accordance with. the compact; and the lands, for costs of entry, *etc.*, were registered for the nominal fee of ten dollars per thousand acres. But as the Transylvania Company was never able to secure a "satisfactory and indisputable title," the clause resulted in perpetual nonpayment. In 1783, following the lead of Virginia in the case of Transylvania, North Carolina declared the Transylvania Company's purchase void, but granted the company in compensation a tract of one hundred and ninety thousand acres in Powell's Valley. As compensation, the grants of North Carolina and Virginia were quite inadequate, considering the value of the service in behalf of permanent western colonization rendered by the Transylvania company.

James Robertson was chosen as presiding officer of the court of twelve commissioners, and was also elected commander-in-chief of the military forces of the eight little associated settlements on the Cumberland. Here for the next two years the self-reliant settlers under Robertson's wise and able leadership successfully repelled the Indians in their guerrilla warfare, firmly entrenched themselves in their forest-girt stronghold, and vindicated their claim to the territory by right of occupation and conquest. Here sprang up in later times a great and populous city—named, strangely enough, neither for Henderson, the founder, nor for Robertson and Donelson, the leaders of the two colonizing parties, but for one having no association with its history or origins, the gallant North Carolinian, General Francis Nash, who was killed at the Battle of Germantown.

CHAPTER XVIII. King's Mountain

With the utmost satisfaction I can acquaint you with the sudden and favorable turn of our public affairs. A few days ago destruction hung over our heads. Cornwallis with at least 1500 British and Tories waited at Charlotte for the reinforcement of 1000 from Broad River, which reinforcement has been entirely cut off, 130 killed and the remainder captured. Cornwallis immediately retreated, and is now on his way toward Charleston, with part of our army in his rear . . . .—Elizabeth Maxwell Steel: Salisbury, October 25, 1780.

So thoroughly had the Cherokees been subdued by the devastations of the campaign of 1776 that for several years thereafter they were unable to organize for a new campaign against the backwoodsmen along the frontiers of North Carolina and Tennessee. During these years the Holston settlers principally busied themselves in making their position secure, as well as in setting their house in order by severely punishing the lawless Tory element among them. In 1779 the Chickamaugas, with whom The Dragging Canoe and his irreconcilable followers among the Cherokees had joined hands after the campaign of 1776, grew so bold in their bloody forays upon small exposed settlements that North Carolina and Virginia in conjunction despatched a strong expedition against them. Embarking on April 10th at the mouth of Big Creek near the present Rogersville, Tennessee, three hundred and fifty men led by Colonel Evan Shelby descended the Tennessee to the fastnesses of the Chickamaugas. Meeting with no resistance from the astonished Indians, who fled to the shelter of the densely wooded hills, they laid waste the Indian towns and destroyed the immense stores of goods collected by the British agents for distribution among the red men. The Chickamaugas were completely quelled; and during the period of great stress through which the Tennessee frontiersmen were soon to pass, the Cherokees were restrained through the wise diplomacy of Joseph Martin, Superintendent of Indian affairs for Virginia.

The great British offensive against the Southern colonies, which were regarded as the vulnerable point in the American Confederacy, was fully launched upon the fall of Charleston in May, 1780. Cornwallis established his headquarters at Camden; and one of his lieutenants, the persuasive and brilliant Ferguson, soon rallied thousands of Loyalists in South Carolina to the British standard. When Cornwallis inaugurated his campaign for cutting Washington wholly off from the Southern colonies by invading North Carolina, the men upon the western waters realized that the time had come to rise, in defense of their state and in protection of their homes. Two hundred Tennessee riflemen from Sullivan County, under Colonel Isaac Shelby, were engaged in minor operations in South Carolina conducted by Colonel Charles McDowell; and conspicuous among these engagements was the affair at Musgrove's Mill on August 18th when three hundred horsemen led by Colonel James Williams, a native of Granville County, North Carolina, Colonel Isaac Shelby, and Lieutenant-Colonel Clark of Georgia repulsed with heavy loss a British force of between four and five hundred.

These minor successes availed nothing in face of the disastrous defeat of Gates by Cornwallis at Camden on August 16th and the humiliating blow to Sumter at Rocky Mount on the following day. Ferguson hotly pursued the frontiersmen, who then retreated over the mountains; and from his camp at Gilbert Town he despatched a threatening message to the Western leaders, declaring that if they did not desist from their opposition to the British arms and take protection under his standard, he would march his army over the mountains and lay their country waste with fire and sword. Stung to action, Shelby hastily rode off to consult with Sevier at his log castle near Jonesboro; and together they matured a plan to arouse the mountain men and attack Ferguson by surprise. In the event of failure, these wilderness free-lances planned to leave the country and find a home with the Spaniards in Louisiana.

At the original place of rendezvous, the Sycamore Shoals of the Watauga, the overmountain men gathered on September 25th. There an eloquent sermon was preached to them by that fiery man of God, the Reverend Samuel Doak, who concluded his discourse with a stirring invocation to the sword of the Lord and of Gideon—a sentiment greeted with the loud applause of the militant frontiersmen. Here and at various places along the march they were joined by detachments of border fighters summoned to join the expedition—Colonel William Campbell, who with some reluctance had abandoned his own plans in response to Shelby's urgent and repeated message, in command of four hundred hardy frontiersmen from Washington County, Virginia; Colonel Benjamin Cleveland, with the wild fighters of Wilkes known as "Cleveland's Bulldogs"; Colonel Andrew Hampton, with the stalwart riflemen of Rutherford; Major Joseph Winston, the cousin of Patrick Henry, with the flower of the citizenry of Surry; the McDowells, Charles and Joseph, with the bold borderers of Burke; Colonels Lacy and Hill, with well-trained soldiers of South Carolina; and Brigadier-General James Williams, leading the intrepid Rowan volunteers.

Before breaking camp at Quaker Meadows, the leading officers in conference chose Colonel William Campbell as temporary officer of the day, until they could secure a general officer from headquarters as commander-in-chief. The object of the mountaineers and big-game hunters was, in their own terms, to pursue Ferguson, to run him down, and to capture him. In pursuance of this plan, the leaders on arriving at the ford of Green River chose out a force of six hundred men, with the best mounts and equipment; and at daybreak on October 6th this force of picked mounted riflemen, followed by some fifty "foot-cavalry" eager to join in the pursuit, pushed rapidly on to the Cowpens. Here a second selection took place; and Colonel Campbell, was again elected commander of the detachment, now numbering some nine hundred and ten horsemen and eighty odd footmen, which dashed rapidly on in pursuit of Ferguson.

The British commander had been apprised of the coming of the over-mountain men. Scorning to make a forced march and attempt to effect a junction with Cornwallis at Charlotte, Ferguson chose to make a stand and dispose once for all of the barbarian horde whom he denounced as mongrels and the dregs of mankind. After despatching to Cornwallis a message asking for aid, Ferguson took up his camp on King's

Mountain, just south of the North Carolina border line, in the present York County, South Carolina. Here, after his pickets had been captured in silence, he was surprised by his opponents. At three o'clock in the afternoon of October 7th the mountain hunters treed their game upon the heights.

The battle which ensued presents an extraordinary contrast in the character of the combatants and the nature of the strategy and tactics. Each party ran true to form— Ferguson repeating Braddock's suicidal policy of opposing bayonet charges to the deadly fusillade of riflemen, who in Indian fashion were carefully posted behind trees and every shelter afforded by the natural inequalities of the ground. In the army of the Carolina and Virginia frontiersmen, composed of independent detachments recruited from many sources and solicitous for their own individual credit, each command was directed in the battle by its own leader. Campbell—like Cleveland, Winston, Williams, Lacey, Shelby, McDowell, Sevier, and Hambright— personally led his own division; but the nature of the fighting and the peculiarity of the terrain made it impossible for him, though the chosen commander of the expedition, actually to play that rôle in the battle. The plan agreed upon in advance by the frontier leaders was simple enough—to surround and capture Ferguson's camp on the high plateau. The more experienced Indian fighters, Sevier and Shelby, unquestionably suggested the general scheme which in any case would doubtless have been employed by the frontiersmen; it was to give the British "Indian play"— namely to take cover everywhere and to fire from natural shelter. Cleveland, a Hercules in strength and courage who had fought the Indians and recognized the wisdom of Indian tactics, ordered his men, as did some of the other leaders, to give way before a bayonet charge, but to return to the attack after the charge had spent its force.

"My brave fellows," said Cleveland, "every man must consider himself an officer, and act from his own judgment. Fire as quick as you can, and stand your ground as long as you can. When you can do no better, get behind trees, or retreat; but I beg you not to run quite off. If we are repulsed, let us make a point of returning and renewing the fight; perhaps we may have better luck in the second attempt than in the first."

The plateau upon which Ferguson was encamped was the top of an eminence some six hundred yards long and about two hundred and fifty yards from one base across to the other; and its shape was that of an Indian paddle, varying from one hundred and twenty yards at the blade to sixty yards at the handle in width. Outcropping boulders upon the outer edge of the plateau afforded some slight shelter for Ferguson's force; but, unsuspicious of attack, Ferguson had made no abatis to protect his camp from the assault to which it was so vulnerable because of the protection of the timber surrounding it on all sides. As to the disposition of the attacking force, the center to the northeast was occupied by Cleveland with his "Bulldogs," Hambright with his South Fork Boys from the Catawba (now Lincoln County, North Carolina), and Winston with his Surry riflemen; to the south were the divisions of Joseph McDowell, Sevier, and Campbell; while Lacey's South Carolinians, the Rowan levies under Williams, and the Watauga borderers under Shelby were stationed upon the north side. Ferguson's forces consisted of Provincial Rangers, one hundred and fifty strong, and other well-drilled Loyalists, between eight and nine hundred in number; but his strength was seriously weakened by the absence of a foraging party of between one and two hundred who had gone off on the morning the battle occurred. Shelby's men, before getting into position, received a hot fire, the opening shots of the engagement. This inspired Campbell, who now threw off his coat, to shout encouraging orders to his men posted on the side of the mountain opposite to Shelby's force. When Campbell's Virginians uttered a series of piercing shouts, the British officer, De Peyster, second in command, remarked to his chief: "These things are ominous—these are the damned yelling boys."

The battle, which lasted some minutes short of an hour, was waged with terrific ferocity. The Loyalist militia, whenever possible, fired from the shelter of the rocks; while the Provincial Corps, with fixed bayonets, steadily charged the frontiersmen, who fired at close range and then rapidly withdrew to the very base of the mountain. After each bayonet charge the Provincials coolly withdrew to the summit, under the accumulating fire of the returning mountaineers, who quickly gathered in their rear. Owing to their elevated location, the British, although using the rapid-fire breech-loading rifle invented by Ferguson himself, found their vision deflected, and continually fired high, thus suffering from nature's handicap, refraction. The militia, using sharpened butcher-knives which Ferguson had taught them to utilize as bayonets, charged against the mountaineers; but their fire, in answer to the deadly fusillade of the expert squirrel-shooters, was belated, owing to the fact that they could not fire while the crudely improvised bayonets remained inserted in their pieces. The Americans, continually firing upward, found ready marks for their aim in the clearly delineated outlines of their adversaries, and felt the fierce exultation which animates the hunter who has tracked to its lair and surrounded wild game at bay.

The leaders of the various divisions of the mountaineers bore themselves with impetuous bravery, recklessly rushing between the lines of fire and with native eloquence, interspersed with profanity, rallying their individual commands again and again to the attack. The valiant Campbell scaled the rugged heights, loudly encouraging his men to the ascent. Cleveland, resolutely facing the foe, urged on is Bulldogs with the inspiriting words: "Come, boys; let's try 'em again. We'll have better luck next time." No sooner did Shelby's men reach the bottom of the hill, in retreating before a charge, than their commander, fiery and strenuous, ardently shouted: "Now boys, quickly reload your rifles, and let's advance upon them, and give them another hell of a fire." The most deadly charge, led by De Peyster himself, fell upon Hambright's South Fork boys; and one of their gallant officers, Major Chronicle, waving his military hat, was mortally wounded, the command, "Face to the hill!", dying on his lips. These veteran soldiers, unlike the mountaineers, firmly met the shock of the charge, and a number of their men were shot down or transfixed; but the remainder, reserving their fire until the charging column was only a few feet away, poured in a deadly volley before retiring. The gallant William Lenoir, whose reckless bravery made him a conspicuous target for the enemy, received several wounds and emerged from the battle with his hair and clothes torn by balls. The ranking American officer, Brigadier General James

104

Williams, was mortally wounded while "on the very top of the mountain, in the thickest of the fight"; and as he momentarily revived, his first words were: "For God's sake, boys, don't give up the hill." Hambright, sorely wounded, his boot overflowing with blood and his hat riddled with three bullet holes, declined to dismount, but pressed gallantly forward, exclaiming in his "Pennsylvania Dutch": "Huzza, my prave poys, fight on a few minutes more, and the pattle will be over!" On the British side, Ferguson was supremely valorous, rapidly dashing from one point to another, rallying his men, oblivious to all danger. Wherever the shrill note of his silver whistle sounded, there the fighting was hottest and the British resistance the most stubborn. His officers fought with the characteristic steadiness of the British soldier; and again and again his men charged headlong against the wavering and fiery circle of the frontiersmen.

Ferguson's boast that "he was on King's Mountain, that he was king of the Mountain, and God Almighty could not drive him from it" was doubtless prompted, less by a belief in the impregnability of his position, than by a desperate desire to inspire confidence in his men. His location was admirably chosen for defense against attack by troops employing regulation tactics; but, never dreaming of the possibility of sudden investment, Ferguson had erected no fortifications for his encampment. His frenzied efforts on the battlefield seem like a mad rush against fate; for the place was indefensible against the peculiar tactics of the frontiersmen. While the mountain flamed like a volcano and resounded with the thunder of the guns, a steady stricture was in progress. The lines were drawn tighter and tighter around the trapped and frantically struggling army; and at last the fall of their commander, riddled with bullets, proved the tragic futility of further resistance. The game was caught and bagged to a man. When Winston, with his fox-hunters of Surry, dashed recklessly through the woods, says a chronicler of the battle, and the last to come into position,

Flow'd in, and settling, circled all the lists,

then

From all the circle of the hills death sleeted in upon the doomed.

The battle was decisive in its effect—shattering the plans of Cornwallis, which till then appeared certain of success. The victory put a full stop to the invasion of North Carolina, which was then well under way. Cornwallis abandoned his carefully prepared campaign and immediately left the state. After ruthlessly hanging nine prisoners, an action which had an effectively deterrent effect upon future Tory murders and depredations, the patriot force quietly disbanded. The brilliant initiative of the buckskin-clad borderers, the strenuous energy of their pursuit, the perfection of their surprise—all reinforced by the employment of ideal tactics for meeting the given situation—were the controlling factors in this overwhelming victory of the Revolution. The pioneers of the Old Southwest—the independent and aggressive yeomanry of North Carolina, Virginia, and South Carolina—had risen in their might. Without the aid or authority of blundering state governments, they had created an army of frontiersmen, Indian-fighters, and big-game hunters which had found no parallel or equal on the continent since the Battle of the Great Kanawha.

CHAPTER XIX. The State of Franklin

Designs of a more dangerous nature and deeper die seem to glare in the western revolt .... I have thought proper to issue this manifesto, hereby warning all persons concerned in the said revolt . . . that the honour of this State has been particularly wounded, by seizing that by violence which, in time, no doubt, would have been obtained by consent, when the terms of separation would have been explained or stipulated, to the mutual sat'isfaction of the mother and new State . . . . Let your proposals be consistent with the honour of the State to accede to, which by your allegiance as good citizens, you cannot violate and I make no doubt but her generosity, in time, will meet your wishes.—Governor Alexander Martin: Manifesto against the State of Franklin, April 25, 1785.

To the shrewd diplomacy of Joseph Martin, who held the Cherokees in check during the period of the King's Mountain campaign, the settlers in the valleys of the Watauga and the Holston owed their temporary immunity from Indian attack. But no sooner did Sevier and his over-mountain men return from the battle-field of King's Mountain than they were called upon to join in an expedition against the Cherokees, who had again gone on the war-path at the instigation of the British. After Sevier with his command had defeated a small party of Indians at Boyd's Creek in December, the entire force of seven hundred riflemen, under the command of Colonel Arthur Campbell, with Major Joseph Martin as subordinate, penetrated to the heart of the Indian country, burned Echota, Chilhowee, Settiquo, Hiawassee, and seven other principal villages, and destroyed an immense amount of property and supplies. In March, suspecting that the arch-conspirators against the white settlers were the Cherokees at the head waters of the Little Tennessee, Sevier led one hundred and fifty horsemen through the devious mountain defiles and struck the Indians a swift and unexpected blow at Tuckasegee, near the present Webster, North Carolina. In this extraordinarily daring raid, one of his most brilliant feats of arms, Sevier lost only one man killed and one wounded; while upon the enemy he inflicted the loss of thirty killed, took many more prisoners, burned six Indian towns, and captured many horses and supplies. Once his deadly work was done, Sevier with his bold cavaliers silently plunged again into the forest whence he had so suddenly emerged, and returned in triumph to the settlements.

Disheartened though the Indians were to see the smoke of their burning towns, they sullenly remained averse to peace; and they did not keep the treaty made at Long Island in July, 1781. The Indians suffered from very real grievances at the hands of the lawless white settlers who persisted in encroaching upon the Indian lands. When the Indian ravages were resumed, Sevier and Anderson, the latter from Sullivan County, led a punitive expedition of two hundred riflemen against the Creeks and the Chickamaugas; and employing the customary tactics of laying waste the Indian towns, administered stern and salutary chastisement to the copper-colored marauders.

During this same period the settlers on the Cumberland were displaying a grim fortitude and stoical endurance in the face of Indian attack forever memorable in the history of the Old Southwest. On the night of January 15, 1781, the settlers at Freeland's Station, after a desperate resistance, succeeded in beating off the savages who attacked in force. At Nashborough on April 2d, twenty of the settlers were lured from the stockade by the artful wiles of the savages; and it was only after serious loss that they finally won their way back to the protection of the fort. Indeed, their return was due to the fierce dogs of the settlers, which were released at the most critical moment, and attacked the astounded Indians with such ferocity that the diversion thus created enabled the settlers to escape from the deadly trap. During the next two years the history of the Cumberland settlements is but the gruesome recital of murder after murder of the whites, a few at a time, by the lurking Indian foe. Robertson's dominant influence alone prevented the abandonment of the sorely harassed little stations. The arrival of the North Carolina commissioners for the purpose of laying off bounty lands and settlers' preemptions, and the treaty of peace concluded at the French Lick on November 5 and 6, 1783, gave permanence and stability to the Cumberland settlements. The lasting friendship of the Chickasaws was won; but the Creeks for some time continued to harass the Tennessee pioneers. The frontiersmen's most formidable foe, the Cherokees, stoically, heroically fighting the whites in the field, and smallpox, syphilis, and drunkenness at home, at last abandoned the unequal battle. The treaty at Hopewell on November 28, 1785, marks the end of an era—the Spartan yet hopeless resistance of the intrepid red men to the relentless and frequently unwarranted expropriation by the whites of the ancient and immemorial domain of the savage.

The skill in self-government of the isolated people beyond the mountains, and the ability they had already demonstrated in the organization of "associations," received a strong stimulus on June 2, 1784, when the legislature of North Carolina ceded to the Congress of the United States the title which that state possessed to the land west of the Alleghanies. Among the terms of the Cession Act were these conditions: that the ceded territory should be formed into a separate state or states; and that if Congress should not accept the lands thus ceded and give due notice within two years, the act should be of no force and the lands should revert to North Carolina. No sooner did this news reach the Western settlers than they began to mature plans for the organization of a government during the intervening twelve months. Their exposed condition on the frontiers, still harassed by the Indians, and North Carolina's delay in sending goods promised the Indians by a former treaty, both promoted Indian hostility; and these facts, combined with their remote location beyond the mountains, rendering them almost inaccessible to communication with North Carolina—all rendered the decision of the settlers almost inevitable. Moreover, the allurements of high office and the dazzling dreams of ambition were additional motives sufficiently human in themselves to give driving power to the movement toward independence.

At a convention assembled at Jonesborough on August 23, 1784, delegates from the counties of Washington, Sullivan, and Greene characteristically decided to organize an "Association." They solemnly declared by resolution: "We have a just and undeniable right to petition to Congress to accept the session made by North Carolina, and for that body to countenance us for forming ourselves into a separate government, and to frame either a permanent or temporary constitution, agreeably to a resolve of Congress . . . ." Meanwhile, Governor Martin, largely as the result of the prudent advice of North Carolina's representative in Congress, Dr. Hugh Williamson, was brought to the conclusion that North Carolina, in the passage of the cession act, had acted precipitately. This important step had been taken without the full consideration of the people of the state. Among the various arguments advanced by Williamson was the impressive contention that, in accordance with the procedure in the case of other states, the whole expense of the huge Indian expeditions in 1776 and the heavy militia aids to South Carolina and Georgia should be credited to North Carolina as partial fulfilment of her continental obligations before the cession should be irrevocably made to the Federal government. Williamson's arguments proved convincing; and it was thus primarily for economic reasons of far reaching national importance that the assembly of North Carolina (October 22 to November 25, 1784) repealed the cession act made the preceding spring.

Before the news of the repeal of the cession act could reach the western waters, a second convention met at Jonesborough on December 17th. Sentiment at this time was much divided, for a number of the people, expecting the repeal of the cession act, genuinely desired a continued allegiance to North Carolina. Of these may well have been John Sevier, who afterward declared to Joseph Martin that he had been "Draged into the Franklin measures by a large number of the people of this country." The principal act of this convention was the adoption of a temporary constitution for six months and the provision for a convention to be held within one year, at the expiration of which time this constitution should be altered, or adopted as the permanent constitution of the new state. The scholars on the western waters, desiring to commemorate their aspirations for freedom, chose as the name of the projected new state: "Frankland"—the Land of the Free. The name finally chosen, however, perhaps for reasons of policy, was "Franklin," in honor of Benjamin Franklin. Meanwhile, in order to meet the pressing needs for a stable government along the Tennessee frontier, the North Carolina assembly, which repealed the cession act, created out of the four western counties the District of Washington, with John Haywood as presiding judge and David Campbell as associate, and conferred upon John Sevier the rank of brigadier general of the new district. The first week in December Governor Martin sent to Sevier his military commission; and replying to Joseph Martin's query (December 31, 1784, prompted by Governor Martin) as to whether, in view of the repeal of the cession act, he intended to persist in revolt or await developments, Sevier gave it out broadcast that "we shall pursue no further measures as to a new State."

Owing to the remoteness of the Tennessee settlements and the difficulty of appreciating through correspondence the atmosphere of sentiment in Franklin, Governor Martin realized the necessity of sending a personal representative to discover the true state of affairs in the disaffected region beyond the mountains. For the post of ambassador to the new government, Governor Martin selected a man distinguished for mentality and diplomatic skill, a pioneer of Tennessee and Kentucky, Judge Richard Henderson's brother, Colonel Samuel Henderson. Despite Sevier's disavowal of any further intention to establish a new state, the governor gave Colonel Henderson elaborate written instructions, the purport of which was to learn all that he could about the political complexion of the Tennessee frontiersmen, the sense of the people, and the agitation for a separate commonwealth. Moreover, in the hope of placating the leading chieftains of the Cherokees, who had bitterly protested against the continued aggressions and encroachments upon their lands by the lawless borderers, he instructed Colonel Henderson also to learn the temper and dispositions of the Indians, and to investigate the case of Colonel James Hubbardt who was charged with the murder of Untoola of Settiquo, a chief of the Cherokees.

When Colonel Henderson arrived at Jonesborough, he found the third Franklin legislature in session, and to this body he presented Governor Martin's letter of February 27, 1785. In response to the governor's request for an "account of the late proceedings of the people in the western country," an extended reply was drafted by the new legislature; and this letter, conveyed to Governor Martin by Colonel Henderson, in setting forth in detail the reasons for the secession, made the following significant statement: "We humbly thank North Carolina for every sentiment of regard she has for us, but are sorry to observe, that as it is founded upon principles of interest, as is aparent from the tenor of your letter, we are doubtful, when the cause ceases which is the basis of that affection, we shall lose your esteem." At the same time (March 22nd), Sevier, who had just been chosen Governor of the State of Franklin, transmitted to Governor Martin by Colonel Henderson a long letter, not hitherto published in any history of the period, in which he outspokenly says:

"It gives me great pain to think there should arise any Disputes between us and North Carolina, & I flatter myself when North Carolina states the matter in a fair light she will be fully convinced that necessity and self preservation have Compelled Us to the measures we Have taken, and could the people have discovered that No. Carolina would Have protected and Govern'd them, They would have remained where they were; but they perceived a neglect and Coolness, and the Language of Many of your most leading members Convinced them they were Altogether Disregarded."

Following the issuance of vigorous manifestos by Martin (April 25th) and Sevier (May 15th), the burden of the problem fell upon Richard Caswell, who in June succeeded Martin as Governor of North Carolina.

Meantime the legislature of the over-mountain men had given the name of Franklin to the new state, although for some time it continued to be called by many Frankland, and its adherents Franks. The legislature had also established an academy named after Governor Martin, and had appointed (March 12th) William Cocke as a delegate to the Continental Congress, urging its acceptance of the cession. In the Memorial from the Franklin legislature to the Continental Congress, dealing in some detail with North Carolina's failure to send the Cherokees some goods promised them for lands acquired by treaty, it is alleged:

"She [North Carolina] immediately stoped the goods she had promised to give the Indians for the said land which so exasperated them that they begun to commit hostalities on our frontiers in this situation we were induced to a declaration of Independence not doubting we should be excused by Congress . . . as North Carolina seemed quite regardless of our interest and the Indians daily murdering our friends and relations without distinction of age or sex."

Sympathizing with the precarious situation of the settlers, as well as desiring the cession, Congress urged North Carolina to amend the repealing act and execute a conveyance of the western territory to the Union.

Among the noteworthy features of the Franklin movement was the constitution prepared by a committee, headed by the Reverend Samuel Houston of Washington County, and presented at the meeting of the Franklin legislature, Greeneville, November 14, 1785. This eccentric constitution was based in considerable part upon the North Carolina model; but it was "rejected in the lump" and the constitution of North Carolina, almost unchanged, was adopted. Under this Houston constitution, the name "Frankland" was chosen for the new state. The legislature was to consist of but a single house. In a section excluding from the legislature "ministers of the gospel, attorneys at law, and doctors of physics," those were declared ineligible for office who were of immoral character or guilty of "such flagrant enormities as drunkenness, gaming, profane swearing, lewdness, Sabbath-breaking and such like," or who should deny the existence of God, of heaven, and of hell, the inspiration of the Scriptures, or the existence of the Trinity. Full religious liberty and the rights of conscience were assured—but strict orthodoxy was a condition for eligibility to office. No one should be chosen to office who was "not a scholar to do the business." This remarkable document, which provided for many other curious innovations in government, was the work of pioneer doctrinaires—Houston, Campbell, Cocke, and Tipton—and deserves study as a bizarre reflection of the spirit and genius of the western frontiersmen.

The liberal policy of Martin, followed by the no less conciliatory attitude of his successor, Caswell, for the time proved wholly abortive. However, Martin's appointment of Evan Shelby in Sevier's place as brigadier, and of Jonathan Tipton as colonel of his county, produced disaffection among the Franks; and the influence of Joseph Martin against the new government was a powerful obstacle to its success. At first the two sets of military, civil, and judicial officers were able to work amicably together; and a working-basis drawn up by Shelby and Sevier, although afterward repudiated by the Franklin legislature, smoothed over some of the rapidly accumulating difficulties. The persistent and quiet assertion of authority by North Carolina, without any overt act of violence against the officers of Franklin state, revealed great diplomatic skill in Governors Martin and Caswell. It was doubtless the considerate policy of the latter, coupled with the defection from Sevier's cause of men of the stamp of Houston and Tipton, after the blundering and cavalier rejection of their singular constitution, which undermined the foundations of Franklin. Sevier himself later wrote with considerable bitterness: "I have been faithfull, and my own breast acquits myself that I have acted no part but what has been Consistent with honor and justice, tempered with Clemency and mercy. How far our pretended patriots have supported me as their pretended chiefe magistrate, I leave the world at large to Judge." Arthur Campbell's plans for the formation of a greater Franklin, through the union of the people on the western waters of Virginia with those of

North Carolina, came to nought when Virginia in the autumn of 1785 with stern decisiveness passed an act making it high treason to erect an independent government within her limits unless authorized by the assembly. Sevier, however, became more fixed in his determination to establish a free state, writing to Governor Caswell: "We shall continue to act independent and would rather suffer death, in all its various and frightful shapes, than conform to anything that is disgraceful." North Carolina, now proceeding with vigor (November, 1786), fully reassumed its sovereignty and jurisdiction over the mountain counties, but passed an act of pardon and oblivion, and in many ways adopted moderate and conciliatory measures.

Driven to extremities, Cocke and Sevier in turn appealed for aid and advice to Benjamin Franklin, in whose honor the new state had been named. In response to Cocke, Franklin wrote (August 12, 1786): "I think you are perfectly right in resolving to submit them [the Points in Dispute] to the Decision of Congress and to abide by their Determination." Franklin's views change in the interim; for when, almost a year later, Sevier asks him for counsel, Franklin has come to the conclusion that the wisest move for Sevier was not to appeal to Congress, but to endeavor to effect some satisfactory compromise with North Carolina (June 30, 1787):

"There are only two Things that Humanity induces me to wish you may succeed in: The Accomodating your Misunderstanding with the Government of North Carolina, by amicable Means; and the Avoiding an Indian war, by preventing Encroaching on their Lands . . . . The Inconvenience to your People attending so remote a Seat of Government, and the difficulty to that Government in ruling well so remote a People, would I think be powerful Inducements with it, to accede to any fair & reasonable Proposition it may receive from you towards an Accommodation."

Despite Sevier's frenzied efforts to achieve independence—his treaty with the Indians, his sensational plan to incorporate the Cherokees into the new state, his constancy to an ideal of revolt against others in face of the reality of revolt against himself, his struggle, equivocal and half-hearted, with the North Carolina authorities under Tipton—despite all these heroic efforts, the star of Franklin swiftly declined. The vigorous measures pursued by General Joseph Martin, and his effective influence focussed upon a movement already honey-combed with disaffection, finally turned the scale. To the Franklin leaders he sent the urgent message: "Nothing will do but a submission to the laws of North Carolina." Early in April, 1788, Martin wrote to Governor Randolph of Virginia: "I returned last evening from Green Co. Washington destrict, North Carolina, after a tower through that Co'ntry, and am happy to inform your Excellency that the late unhappy dispute between the State of North Carolina, and the pretended State of Franklin is subsided." Ever brave, constant, and loyal to the interest of the pioneers, Sevier had originally been drawn into the movement against his best judgment. Caught in the unique trap, created by the passage of the cession act and the sudden volte-face of its repeal, he struggled desperately to extricate himself. Alone of all the leaders, the governor of ill-starred Franklin remained recalcitrant.

112

CHAPTER XX. The Lure of Spain—The Haven of Statehood

The people of this region have come to realize truly upon what part of the world and upon which nation their future happiness and security depend, and they immediately infer that their interest and prosperity depend entirely upon the protection and liberality of your government.—John Sevier to Don Diego de Gardoqui, September 12, 1788.

From the early settlements in the eastern parts of this Continent to the late & more recent settlements on the Kentucky in the Rest the same difficulties have constantly occurred which now oppress you, but by a series of patient sufferings, manly and spirited exertions and unconquerable perseverance, they have been altogether or in great measure subdued.—Governor Samuel Johnston to James Robertson and Anthony Bledsoe, January 29, 1788.

A strange sham-battle, staged like some scene from opera bouffe, in the bleak snow-storm of February, 1788, is really the prelude to a remarkable drama of revolt in which Sevier, Robertson, Bledsoe, and the Cumberland stalwarts play the leading roles. On February 27th, incensed beyond measure by the action of Colonel John Tipton in harboring some of his slaves seized by the sheriff under an execution issued by one of the North Carolina courts, Sevier with one hundred and fifty adherents besieged Tipton with a few of his friends in his home on Sinking Creek. The siege was raised at daybreak on February 29th by the arrival of reinforcements under Colonel Maxwell from Sullivan County; and Sevier, who was unwilling to precipitate a conflict, withdrew his forces after some desultory firing, in which two men were killed and several wounded. Soon afterward Sevier sent word to Tipton that on condition his life be spared he would submit to North Carolina. On this note of tragi-comedy the State of Franklin appeared quietly to expire. The usually sanguine Sevier, now thoroughly chastened, sought shelter in the distant settlements— deeply despondent over the humiliating failure of his plans and the even more depressing defection of his erstwhile friends and supporters The revolutionary designs and separatist tendencies which he still harbored were soon to involve him in a secret conspiracy to give over the State of Franklin into the protection of a foreign power.

The fame of Sevier's martial exploits and of his bold stroke for independence had long since gone abroad, astounding even so famous an advocate of liberty as Patrick Henry and winning the sympathy of the Continental Congress. One of the most interested observers of the progress of affairs in the State of Franklin was Don Diego de Gardoqui, who had come to America in the spring of 1785, bearing a commission to the American Congress as Spanish charge d'affaires (Encargados de Negocios) to the United States. In the course of his negotiations with Jay concerning the right of navigation of the Mississippi River, which Spain denied to the Americans, Gardoqui was not long in discovering the violent resentment of the Western frontiersmen, provoked by Jay's crass blunder in proposing that the American republic, in return for reciprocal foreign advantages offered by Spain, should waive for twenty-five years her right to navigate the Mississippi. The Cumberland traders had already felt the heavy hand of Spain in the confiscation of their goods at Natchez; but thus far the leaders of the Tennessee frontiersmen had prudently restrained the more turbulent agitators against the Spanish policy, fearing lest the spirit of retaliation, once aroused, might know no bounds. Throughout the entire region of the trans-Alleghany, a feeling of discontent and unrest prevailed—quite as much the result of dissatisfaction with the central government which permitted the wholesale restraint of trade, as of resentment against the domination of Spain.

No sooner had the shrewd and watchful Gardoqui, who was eager to utilize the separatist sentiment of the western settlements in the interest of his country, learned of Sevier's armed insurrection against the authority of North Carolina than he despatched an emissary to sound the leading men of Franklin and the Cumberland settlements in regard to an alliance. This secret emissary was Dr. James White, who had been appointed by the United States Government as Superintendent of Indian Affairs for the Southern Department on November 29, 1786. Reporting as instructed to Don Estevan Miro, governor of Louisiana, White, the corrupt tool of Spain, stated concerning his confidential mission that the leaders of "Frankland" and "Cumberland district" had "eagerly accepted the conditions" laid down by Gardoqui: to take the oath of allegiance to Spain, and to renounce all submission or allegiance whatever to any other sovereign or power. Satisfied by the secret advices received, the Spanish minister reported to the home authorities his confident belief that the Tennessee backwoodsmen, if diplomatically handled, would readily throw in their lot with Spain.

After the fiasco of his siege of Tipton's home, Sevier had seized upon the renewal of hostilities by the Cherokees as a means of regaining his popularity. This he counted upon doing by rallying his old comrades-in-arms under his standard and making one of his meteoric, whirlwind onslaughts upon their ancient Indian foe. The victory of this erstwhile popular hero, the beloved "Nolichucky Jack of the Border," over the Indians at a town on the Hiwassee "so raised him in the esteem of the people on the frontier," reports Colonel Maxwell, "that the people began [once more] to flock to his standard." Inspirited by this good turn in his fortunes, Sevier readily responded to Dr. White's overtures.

Alarmed early in the year over the unprovoked depredations and murders by the Indians in several Tennessee counties and on the Kentucky road, Sevier, Robertson, and Anthony Bledsoe had persuaded Governor Samuel Johnston of North Carolina to address Gardoqui and request him to exert his influence to prevent further acts of savage barbarity. In letters to Governor Johnston, to Robertson, and to Sevier, all of date April 18th, Gardoqui expressed himself in general as being "extremely surprised to know that there is a suspicion that the good government of Spain is encouraging these acts of barbarity." The letters to Robertson and Sevier, read between the lines as suggestive reinforcements of Spain's secret proposals, possess real significance. The letter to Sevier contains this dexterously expressed sentiment: "His Majesty is very favorably inclined to give the inhabitants of that region all the protection that they ask for and, on my part, I shall take very great pleasure in contributing to it on this occasion and other occasions."

114

This letter, coupled with the confidential proposals of Dr. White, furnished a convenient opening for correspondence with the Spaniards; and in July Sevier wrote to Gardoqui indicating his readiness to accede to their proposals. After secret conferences with men who had supported him throughout the vicissitudes of his ill-starred state, Sevier carefully matured his plans. The remarkable letter of great length which he wrote to Gardoqui on September 12, 1788, reveals the conspiracy in all its details and presents in vivid colors the strong separatist sentiment of the day. Sevier urgently petitions Gardoqui for the loan of a few thousand pounds, to enable him to "make the most expedient and necessary preparations for defense"; and offers to repay the loan within a short time "by sending the products of this region to the lower ports." Upon the vital matter of "delivering" the State of Franklin to Spain, he forthrightly says:

"Since my last of the 18th of July, upon consulting with the principal men of this country, I have been particularly happy to find that they are equally disposed and ready as I am to accept your propositions and guarantees. You may be sure that the pleasing hopes and ideas which the people of this country hold with regard to the probability of an alliance with, and commercial concessions from, you are very ardent, and that we are unanimously determined on that score. The people of this region have come to realize truly upon what part of the world and upon which nation their future happiness and security depend, and they immediately infer that their interest and prosperity depend entirely upon the protection and liberality of your government. . . . Being the first from this side of the Appalachian Mountains to resort in this way to your protection and liberality, we feel encouraged to entertain the greatest hope that we shall be granted all reasonable aid by him who is so amply able to do it, and to give the protection and help that is asked of him in this petition. You know our delicate situation and the difficulties in which we are in respect to our mother State which is making use of every strategem to impede the development and prosperity of this country . . . . Before I conclude, it may be necessary to remind you that there will be no more favorable occasion than the present one to put this plan into execution. North Carolina has rejected the Constitution and moreover it seems to me that a considerable time will elapse before she becomes a member of the Union, if that event ever happens."

Through Miro, Gardoqui was simultaneously conducting a similar correspondence with General James Wilkinson. The object of the Spanish conspiracy, matured as the result of this correspondence, was to seduce Kentucky from her allegiance to the United States. Despite the superficial similarity between the situation of Franklin and Kentucky, it would be doing Sevier and his adherents a capital injustice to place them in the category of the corrupt Wilkinson and the malodorous Sebastian. Moreover, the secessionists of Franklin, as indicated in the above letter, had the excuse of being left virtually without a country. On the preceding August 1st, North Carolina had rejected the Constitution of the United States; and the leaders of Franklin, who were sorely aggrieved by what they regarded as her indifference and neglect, now felt themselves more than ever out of the Union and wholly repudiated by the mother state. Again, Sevier had the embittered feeling resultant from outlawry. Because of his course in opposing the laws and government of North Carolina and in the killing of several good citizens, including the sheriff of

Washington County, by his forces at Sinking Creek, Sevier, through the action of Governor Johnston of North Carolina, had been attainted of high treason. Under the heavy burden of this grave charge, he felt his hold upon Franklin relax. Further, an atrocity committed in the recent campaign under Sevier's leadership—Kirk's brutal murder of Corn Tassel, a noble old Indian, and other chieftains, while under the protection of a flag of truce—had placed a bar sinister across the fair fame of this stalwart of the border. Utter desperation thus prompted Sevier's acceptance of Gardoqui's offer of the protection of Spain.

John Sevier's son, James, bore the letter of September 12th to Gardoqui. By a strangely ironic coincidence, on the very day (October 10, 1788) that Gardoqui wrote to Miro, recommending to the attention of Spain Dr. White and James Sevier, the emissaries of Franklin, with their plans and proposals, John Sevier was arrested by Colonel Tipton at the Widow Brown's in Washington County, on the charge of high treason. He was handcuffed and borne off, first to Jonesborough and later to Morganton. But his old friends and former comrades-in-arms, Charles and Joseph McDowell, gave bond for his appearance at court; and Morrison, the sheriff, who also had fought at King's Mountain, knocked the irons from his wrists and released him on parole. Soon afterward a number of Sevier's devoted friends, indignant over his arrest, rode across the mountains to Morganton and silently bore him away, never to be arrested again. In November an act of pardon and oblivion with respect to Franklin was passed by the North Carolina Assembly. Although Sevier was forbidden to hold office under the state, the passage of this act automatically operated to clear him of the alleged offense of high treason. With affairs in Franklin taking this turn, it is little wonder that Gardoqui and Miro paid no further heed to Sevier's proposal to accept the protection of Spain. Sevier's continued agitation in behalf of the independence of Franklin inspired Governor Johnston with the fear that he would have to be "proceeded against to the last extremity." But Sevier's opposition finally subsiding, he was pardoned, given a seat in the North Carolina assembly, and with extraordinary consideration honored with his former rank of brigadier-general.

When Dr. White reported to Miro that the leaders of "Frankland" had eagerly accepted Gardoqui's conditions for an alliance with Spain, he categorically added: "With regard to Cumberland district, what I have said of Frankland applies to it with equal force and truth." James Robertson and Anthony Bledsoe had but recently availed themselves of the good offices of Governor Johnston of North Carolina in the effort to influence Gardoqui to quiet the Creek Indians. The sagacious and unscrupulous half breed Alexander McGillivray had placed the Creeks under the protection of Spain in 1784; and shortly afterward they began to be regularly supplied with ammunition by the Spanish authorities. At first Spain pursued the policy of secretly encouraging these Indians to resist the encroachments of the Americans, while she remained on outwardly friendly terms with the United States. During the period of the Spanish conspiracy, however, there is reason to believe that Miro endeavored to keep the Indians at peace with the borderers, as a friendly service, intended to pave the way for the establishment of intimate relations between Spain and the dwellers in the trans-Alleghany. Yet his efforts cannot have been very effective; for the Cumberland settlements continued to suffer from the ravages and depredations of the Creeks, who remained "totally averse to peace, notwithstanding they have had no cause of offence"; and Robertson and Bledsoe reported to Governor Caswell (June 12, 1787): "It is certain, the Chickasaws inform us, that Spanish traders offer a reward for scalps of the Americans." The Indian atrocities became so frequent that Robertson later in the summer headed a party on the famous Coldwater Expedition, in which he severely chastised the marauding Indians. Aroused by the loss of a number of chiefs and warriors at the hands of Robertson's men, and instigated, as was generally believed, by the Spaniards, the Creeks then prosecuted their attacks with renewed violence against the Cumberland settlements.

Unprotected either by the mother state or by the national government, unable to secure free passage to the Gulf for their products, and sorely pressed to defend their homes, now seriously endangered by the incessant attacks of the Creeks, the Cumberland leaders decided to make secret overtures to McGillivray, as well as to communicate to Miro, through Dr. White, their favorable inclination toward the proposals of the one country which promised them protection. In a letter which McGillivray wrote to Miro (transmitted to Madrid, June 15, 1788) in regard to the visit of Messrs. Hackett and Ewing, two trusty messengers sent by Robertson and Bledsoe, he reports that the two delegates from the district of Cumberland had not only submitted to him proposals of peace but "had added that they would throw themselves into the arms of His Majesty as subjects, and that Kentucky and Cumberland are determined to free themselves from their dependence on Congress, because that body can not protect either their property, or favor their commerce, and they therefore believe that they no longer owe obedience to a power which is incapable of protecting them." Commenting upon McGillivray's communication, Miro said in his report to Madrid (June 15, 1788): "I consider as extremely interesting the intelligence conveyed to McGillivray by the deputies on the fermentation existing in Kentucky, with regard to a separation from the Union. Concerning the proposition made to McGillivray by the inhabitants of Cumberland to become the vassals of His Majesty, I have refrained from returning any precise answer."

In his long letter of reply to Robertson and Bledsoe, McGillivray agreed to make peace between his nation, the Creeks, and the Cumberland settlers. This letter was most favorably received and given wide circulation throughout the West. In a most ingratiating reply, offering McGillivray a fine gun and a lot in Nashville, Robertson throws out the following broad suggestion, which he obviously wishes McGillivray to convey to Miro: "In all probability we cannot long remain in our present state, and if the British or any commercial nation who may be in possession of the mouth of the Mississippi would furnish us with trade, and receive our produce there cannot be a doubt but the people on the west side of the Appalachian mountains will open their eyes to their real interest." Robertson actually had the district erected out of the counties of Davidson, Sumner, and Tennessee given the name of "Miro" by the Assembly of North Carolina in November, 1788—a significant symbol of the desires of the Cumberland leaders. In a letter (April 23, 1789), Miro, who had just received letters from Robertson (January 29th) and Daniel Smith (March 4th) postmarked "District of Miro," observes: "The bearer, Fagot, a confidential agent of Gen. Smith, informed me that the inhabitants of Cumberland, or Miro, would ask North Carolina for an act of separation the following fall, and that as soon as this should be obtained other delegates would be sent from Cumberland to New Orleans, with the object of placing that territory under the domination of His Majesty. I replied to both in general terms."

Robertson, Bledsoe, and Smith were successful in keeping secret their correspondence with McGillivray and Miro; and few were in the secret of Sevier's effort to deliver the State of Franklin to Spain. Joseph Martin was less successful in his negotiations; and a great sensation was created throughout the Southern colonies when a private letter from Joseph Martin to McGillivray (November 8, 1788) was intercepted. In this letter Martin said: "I must beg that you write me by the first opportunity in answer to what I am now going to say to you . . . . I hope to do honor to any part of the world I settle in, and am determined to leave the United States, for reasons that I can assign to you when we meet, but durst not trust it to paper." The general assembly of Georgia referred the question of the intercepted letter to the governor of North Carolina (January 24, 1789); and the result was a legislative investigation into Martin's conduct. Eleven months later, the North Carolina assembly exonerated him. From the correspondence of Joseph Martin and Patrick Henry, it would appear that Martin, on Henry's advice, had acted as a spy upon the Spaniards, in order to discover the views of McGillivray, to protect the exposed white settlements from the Indians, and to fathom the designs of the Spaniards against the United States.

The sensational disclosures of Martin's intercepted letter had no deterrent effect upon James Robertson in the attempted execution of his plan for detaching the Cumberland settlements from North Carolina. History has taken no account of the fact that Robertson and the inhabitants now deliberately endeavored to secure an act of separation from North Carolina. In the event of success, the next move planned by the Cumberland leaders, as we have already seen, was to send delegates to New Orleans for the purpose of placing the Cumberland region under the domination of Spain.

A hitherto unknown letter, from Robertson to (Miro), dated Nashville, September 2, 1789, proves that a convention of the people was actually held—the first overt step looking to an alliance with Spain. In this letter Robertson says:

"I must beg your Excellency's permission to take this early opportunity of thanking you for the honor you did me in writing by Mr. White.

"I still hope that your Government, and these Settlements, are destined to be mutually friendly and usefull, the people here are impressed with the necessity of it.

"We have just held a Convention; which has agreed that our members shall insist on being Seperated from North Carolina.

"Unprotected, we are to be obedient to the new Congress of the United States; but we cannot but wish for a more interesting Connection.

118

"The United States afford us no protection. The district of Miro is daily plundered and the inhabitants murdered by the Creeks, and Cherokees, unprovoked.

"For my own part, I conceive highly of the advantages of your Government."

A serious obstacle to the execution of the plans of Robertson and the other leaders of the Cumberland settlements was the prompt action of North Carolina. In actual conformity with the wishes of the Western people, as set forth in the petition of Robertson and Hayes, their representatives, made two years earlier, the legislature of North Carolina in December passed the second act of cession, by which the Western territory of North Carolina was ceded to the United States. Instead of securing an act of separation from North Carolina as the preparatory step to forming what Robertson calls "a more interesting connection" with Spain, Robertson and his associates now found themselves and the transmontane region which they represented flung bodily into the arms of the United States. Despite the unequivocal offer of the calculating and desperate Sevier to "deliver" Franklin to Spain, and the ingenious efforts of Robertson and his associates to place the Cumberland region under the domination of Spain, the Spanish court by its temporizing policy of evasion and indecision definitely relinquished the ready opportunities thereby afforded, of utilizing the powerful separatist tendencies of Tennessee for the purpose of adding the empire upon the Western waters to the Spanish domain in America.

The year 1790 marks the end of an era the heroic age of the pioneers of the Old Southwest. Following the acceptance of North Carolina's deed of cession of her Western lands to the Union (April 2, 1790) the Southwest Territory was erected on May 26th; and William Blount, a North Carolina gentleman of eminence and distinction, was appointed on June 8th to the post of governor of the territory. Two years later (June 1, 1792) Kentucky was admitted into the Union.

It is a remarkable and inspiring circumstance, in testimony of the martial instincts and unwavering loyalty of the transmontane people, that the two men to whom the Western country in great measure owed its preservation, the inciting and flaming spirits of the King's Mountain campaign, were the unopposed first choice of the people as leaders in the trying experiment of Statehood—John Sevier of Tennessee and Isaac Shelby of Kentucky. Had Franklin possessed the patient will of Kentucky, she might well have preceded that region into the Union. It was not, however, until June 1, 1796, that Tennessee, after a romantic and arduous struggle, finally passed through the wide-flung portals into the domain of national statehood.

51550136R00069

Made in the USA
Lexington, KY
27 April 2016